Reflections™

SCRAPBOOKING PROGRAM

Gibbs Smith, Publisher

TO ENRICH AND INSPIRE HUMANKIND

Salt Lake City | Charleston | Santa Fe | Santa Barbara

First Edition

12 11 10 09 08   5 4 3 2 1

Published by
Gibbs Smith, Publisher
P.O. Box 667
Layton, Utah 84041

Orders: 1.800.835.4993
www.gibbs-smith.com

Created By: Jeanette R. Lynton

Executive Director: Kristine Widtfeldt

Creative Manager: Kristy McDonnell

Art Director: Eric Clegg

Project Manager: Stacy San Juan

Writers: JoAnn Jolley, Stephanie Olsen

Copy Editor: Ben Williamson

Production Editors: Adam Cazier, Jeana Goodwin

Design: Kelly Nield, Stephen Hales Creative, Inc.

Production Assistant: Spencer Hales

Photographer: Bradley Slade

Photo Stylist: Anne Smoot

Printed and bound in China

Library of Congress Control Number: 2007936392

ISBN 13: 978-1-4236-0311-5

ISBN 10: 1-4236-0311-7

Thank you to all the talented scrapbook artists who helped make these fabulous layouts come to life.

Reflections Scrapbook Program™ is itself built upon Jeanette R. Lynton's original *ABC Scrapbook Program*® first published in 1999 and the *ABC Scrapbook Program II* published in 2000, as well as the *Reflections Scrapbook Program*™ series *I*, *II*, and *III* published in 2002 and 2003.

For more information about the products used in these layouts, please contact a Close To My Heart Independent Consultant by calling 888-655-6552, or visit www.closetomyheart.com.

Dear Friends:

You may be surprised to know that you are holding my heart in your hands. Yes, it looks like a book, but truthfully, it's the embodiment of many of my sweetest dreams, creative passions, and the roots of a scrapbooking journey that began decades ago when I was just a teenager.

Back then, "scrapbooking" didn't exist. There was just me, my pocket camera, and the memories I cobbled together using dime-store markers, fabric-store notions, and patterns I created from my own imagination.

Many nights, I'd fall asleep in the middle of designing a layout, with photos and embellishments and scraps strewn about my bed. I often joke that my scrapbook slept better than I did, because I couldn't bear to put everything away—instead, I'd just gently crawl under a corner of a blanket or squish myself at the edge of the bed.

The patterns in that original scrapbook form the foundation of *Reflections*™ and the core of scrapbooking itself—10 basic, winning patterns that will never fail you. Some may call them "simple." I think you'll find them *essential*. They work in a variety of combinations and rotations, with common-sense photo sizes, incorporating titles and journaling to tell your story with limitless possibility.

Whether you scrapbook at a table or on your bed as I once did, may *Reflections* wake up your creative spirit and set you on your own journey of the heart. This is more than a book, this is my legacy; this is my heart. This is the foundation of scrapbooking and my gift to you.

Make it from your heart,

Jeanette

Jeanette R. Lynton

JEANETTE R. LYNTON

Since the 1970s, Jeanette has enjoyed a passion for preserving treasured memories, and early in life began creating exclusive stamps and sharing her scrapbooking knowledge. Today, Close To My Heart, the company Jeanette founded, is a leader in the scrapbooking and stamping industry.

Always at the forefront of innovation and creativity, Jeanette's new products have included the world's first true 12" × 12" scrapbooking format; a series of instructional programs offering simple guidelines for dynamic scrapbook layouts and homemade cards; scrapbooking kits featuring pre-printed layouts; and My Acrylix® clear decorative stamps and blocks that allow for perfect stamp placement.

Jeanette's artistic eye and "let me show you how" approach have made scrapbooking faster, simpler, and easier than ever before, while continuing to enhance the art of preserving memories and celebrating relationships.

Great Beginnings Get Even Better

In a very real sense, these pages reflect an enduring legacy of discovery. What began in the early 1970s with my zeal for preserving memories grew into a desire to teach others how to scrapbook, and is now this unique volume. In the late 1990s, my *ABC Scrapbook Program*® was published, with subsequent editions re-titled *Reflections*™ being published in 2002 and 2003. Over the years I have continued to rely on the same 10 foundational patterns you'll find here—Title Topper™, Bottom Border™, Sidebar™, Main Frame™, Front & Center™, Half & Half™, Triple Play™, Quartet™, Treasure Pocket™, and Sampler™—to fashion a wealth of intriguing variations. This is my legacy, and it's now yours to relish and embrace. Enjoy!

Putting it all together: Using *Reflections*™ is like assembling a puzzle with two pieces—except that you get to choose the pieces and the finished look it creates. In this book, many of the featured master or alternate patterns are designed to be your left page in a two-page layout. To get a perfectly balanced, coordinated right page, simply select from the list of companion pages the one that suits your photos and design needs best. In this example, I chose the Reflections: Title Topper—Heading™ master pattern (page 17) for my artwork. Then I selected the Reflections: Sidebar—Original™ pattern (page 40) from the list of recommended companion pages. Each companion page has been carefully coordinated to complement and complete the master pattern you've selected for the left page.

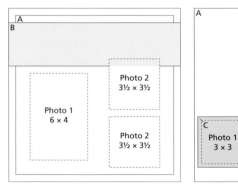

1d. Title Topper—Heading™ (Page 17)

3a. Sidebar—Original™ (Page 40)

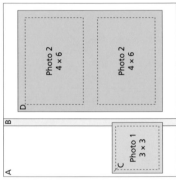

1d. Title Topper—Heading™
Photo Alternate (Page 17)

3a. Sidebar—Original™ (Page 40)
Rotated 90°

Creating perfect combinations: Put the left master pattern and the right companion pattern together for a winning two-page layout: precise design balance, continuity of paper patterns, and proportional photo usage. Perfect results every time!

Rotating is refreshing: For maximum variety in your layouts, experiment using the alternate photo suggestions provided with many of the patterns or rotate your page patterns once or even multiple turns to give your layout perfect balance. In this layout, I've used the exact same pattern combination as shown on the left—but by choosing a different photo option and rotating the patterns, I've created an entirely fresh look!

There's no mystique to great technique. It just takes a little common sense to create uncommonly beautiful layouts. Present your treasured moments using the Reflections: Bottom Border—Footnotes™ pattern (page 31) and its companion pattern, Reflections: Quartet—Pinwheel™ (page 107). Patterns like these in conjunction with a few simple rules of thumb like Finish what you start, and Write on!, will help you create the perfect artistic combination. Now read on to see what I mean.

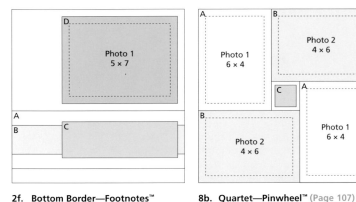

2f. Bottom Border—Footnotes™ (Page 31)

8b. Quartet—Pinwheel™ (Page 107)

2f. Bottom Border—Footnotes™ (Page 31) Rotated 90°

8b. Quartet—Pinwheel™ (Page 107)

Finish what you start: And you'll unify your art. If you mat photos on the left page, mat one or more on the right. If you distress or tear your cardstock, carry the technique over on both pages. Are your photo corners rounded on one page? Then keep that corner rounder handy for your facing page. Use background and texture papers sparingly—but always use a little of the same on both pages of a layout. You'll find that finishing what you start makes for balance—in layouts and life!

Write on! Photos, paper, and embellishments only hint at the story. The names, dates, and precious details are the heart of your layout, so do your artwork "write." A title gives your artwork a visual anchor, and journaling gives it lasting memory. In *Reflections,* you'll find it easy to adapt the patterns to incorporate journaling boxes with ease—and for close-to-the-heart notes or to keep your layout simple and tidy, don't be afraid to use "hidden journaling" tucked inside a pocket, folded on a tag, or secured snugly behind a clip, like a treasure waiting to be discovered.

Title Topper™

1a. Title Topper—
    Subtle
Page 14

1a. Photo Alternate
Page 14

1a. Photo Alternate
Page 14

1b. Title Topper—
    Billboard
Page 15

1b. Photo Alternate
Page 15

1b. Photo Alternate
Page 15

1c. Title Topper—
    Pieced Together
Page 16

1c. Photo Alternate
Page 16

1c. Photo Alternate
Page 16

1d. Title Topper—
    Heading
Page 17

1d. Photo Alternate
Page 17

1d. Photo Alternate
Page 17

1e. Title Topper—
    Equal Portions
Page 18

1e. Photo Alternate
Page 18

1e. Photo Alternate
Page 18

1f. Title Topper—
    Center Focus
Page 19

1f. Photo Alternate
Page 19

1f. Photo Alternate
Page 19

1g. Title Topper—
    Add Up
Page 20

1g. Photo Alternate
Page 20

1g. Photo Alternate
Page 20

1h. Title Topper—
    Photos
Page 21

1h. Photo Alternate
Page 21

1h. Photo Alternate
Page 21

1i. Title Topper—
    Basic
Page 22

1i. Photo Alternate
Page 22

1i. Photo Alternate
Page 22

1j. Title Topper—
    Cover
Page 23

1j. Photo Alternate
Page 23

1j. Photo Alternate
Page 23

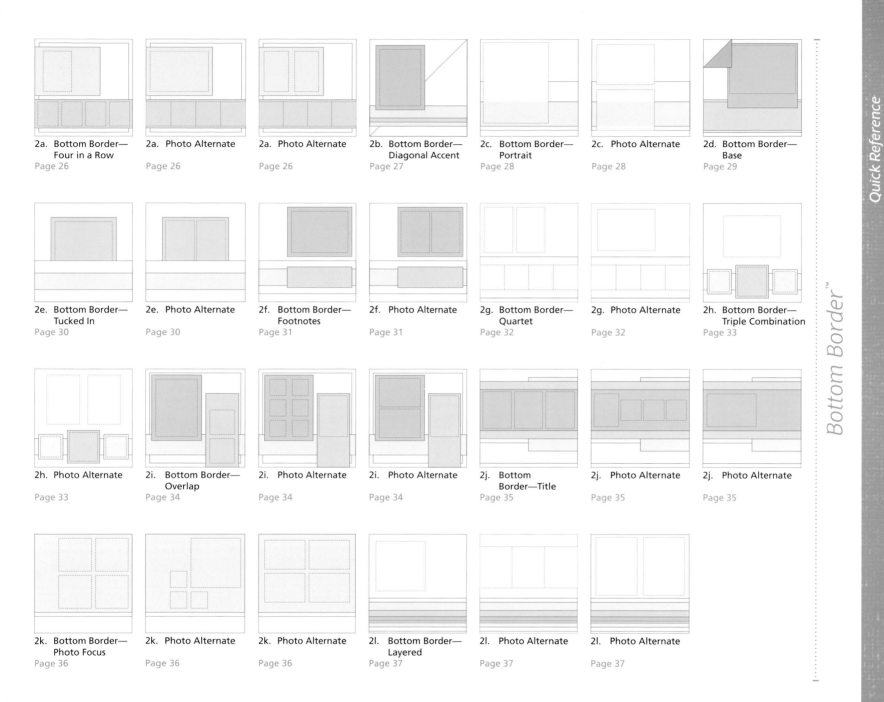

2a. Bottom Border—
Four in a Row
Page 26

2a. Photo Alternate
Page 26

2a. Photo Alternate
Page 26

2b. Bottom Border—
Diagonal Accent
Page 27

2c. Bottom Border—
Portrait
Page 28

2c. Photo Alternate
Page 28

2d. Bottom Border—
Base
Page 29

2e. Bottom Border—
Tucked In
Page 30

2e. Photo Alternate
Page 30

2f. Bottom Border—
Footnotes
Page 31

2f. Photo Alternate
Page 31

2g. Bottom Border—
Quartet
Page 32

2g. Photo Alternate
Page 32

2h. Bottom Border—
Triple Combination
Page 33

2h. Photo Alternate
Page 33

2i. Bottom Border—
Overlap
Page 34

2i. Photo Alternate
Page 34

2i. Photo Alternate
Page 34

2j. Bottom
Border—Title
Page 35

2j. Photo Alternate
Page 35

2j. Photo Alternate
Page 35

2k. Bottom Border—
Photo Focus
Page 36

2k. Photo Alternate
Page 36

2k. Photo Alternate
Page 36

2l. Bottom Border—
Layered
Page 37

2l. Photo Alternate
Page 37

2l. Photo Alternate
Page 37

Bottom Border™

Sidebar™

3a. Sidebar—Original
Page 40

3a. Photo Alternate
Page 40

3a. Photo Alternate
Page 40

3b. Sidebar—Main Frame
Page 41

3b. Photo Alternate
Page 41

3b. Photo Alternate
Page 41

3c. Sidebar—Triple
Page 42

3d. Sidebar—Layers
Page 43

3d. Photo Alternate
Page 43

3d. Photo Alternate
Page 43

3e. Sidebar—Quartet
Page 44

3e. Photo Alternate
Page 44

3e. Photo Alternate
Page 44

3f. Sidebar—Journaling
Page 45

3g. Sidebar—Photo Accent
Page 46

3g. Photo Alternate
Page 46

3g. Photo Alternate
Page 46

3h. Sidebar—Photo Focus
Page 47

3h. Photo Alternate
Page 47

3h. Photo Alternate
Page 47

3i. Sidebar—Balancing Act
Page 48

3i. Photo Alternate
Page 48

3j. Sidebar—Understated
Page 49

Main Frame™

4a. Main Frame—Four Square
Page 52

4b. Main Frame—Quarter Circle
Page 53

4c. Main Frame—Vertical Window
Page 54

4d. Main Frame—Tied Together
Page 55

4e. Main Frame—Charmed
Page 56

4f. Main Frame—Offset
Page 57

4g. Main Frame—Back Drop
Page 58

4h. Main Frame—
Tied Up
Page 59

4i. Main Frame—
Details
Page 60

4j. Main Frame—
Portrait
Page 61

4k. Main Frame—
Quilt Blocks
Page 62

4l. Main Frame—
Perfect Square
Page 63

4m. Main Frame—
Border Cutout
Page 64

4n. Main Frame—
Wrap Around
Page 65

5a. Front & Center—
Blocks
Page 68

5a. Photo Alternate
Page 68

5b. Front & Center—
Space
Page 69

5b. Photo Alternate
Page 69

5b. Photo Alternate
Page 69

5c. Front & Center—
Trio
Page 70

5d. Front & Center—
Focal
Page 71

5d. Photo Alternate
Page 71

5d. Photo Alternate
Page 71

5e. Front & Center—
Split Focus
Page 72

5f. Front & Center—
Mosaic
Page 73

5g. Front & Center—
Accent Band
Page 74

5g. Photo Alternate
Page 74

5g. Photo Alternate
Page 74

5h. Front & Center—
Center Stage
Page 75

5h. Photo Alternate
Page 75

5h. Photo Alternate
Page 75

5i. Front & Center—
In the Middle
Page 76

5j. Front & Center—
Main Idea
Page 77

5j. Photo Alternate
Page 77

5k. Front & Center—
Basic
Page 78

5k. Photo Alternate
Page 78

5k. Photo Alternate
Page 78

5l. Front & Center—
Photo Focus
Page 79

Half & Half

6a. Half & Half—
Corner Title
Page 82

6b. Half & Half—
Split Focus
Page 83

6b. Photo Alternate
Page 83

6c. Half & Half—
Top Focus
Page 84

6d. Half & Half—
Perfect Square
Page 85

6e. Half & Half—Tags
Page 86

6f. Half & Half—
4 Photo
Page 87

6g. Half & Half—
Combination
Page 88

6h. Half & Half—
Balanced
Page 89

6h. Photo Alternate
Page 89

6i. Half & Half—
Simple Frames
Page 90

6j. Half & Half—
It's Sixes
Page 91

Triple Play

7a. Triple Play—
Triple Tagline
Page 94

7b. Triple Play—
Tagline
Page 95

7c. Triple Play—Three
is the Charm
Page 96

7c. Photo Alternate
Page 96

7d. Triple Play—Basic
Page 97

7e. Triple Play—
Offset
Page 98

7f. Triple Play—
Three of a Kind
Page 99

7g. Triple Play—
Columns
Page 100

7g. Photo Alternate
Page 100

7h. Triple Play—
Combination
Page 101

7i. Triple Play—
Foundation
Page 102

7j. Triple Play—
Over the Top
Page 103

Quartet

8a. Quartet—
Border Cutout
Page 106

8a. Photo Alternate
Page 106

8a. Photo Alternate
Page 106

8b. Quartet—
Pinwheel
Page 107

8c. Quartet—
Perfect Square
Page 108

8d. Quartet—Columns
Page 109

8e. Quartet—Panels
Page 110

Quartet™

8e. Photo Alternate
Page 110

8e. Photo Alternate
Page 110

8f. Quartet—Condensed
Page 111

8g. Quartet—Offset
Page 112

8g. Photo Alternate
Page 112

8g. Photo Alternate
Page 112

8h. Quartet—Jigsaw
Page 113

8i. Quartet—In Balance
Page 114

8j. Quartet—Sliding
Page 115

Treasure Pocket™

9a. Treasure Pocket—Basic
Page 118

9b. Treasure Pocket—Main
Page 118

9c. Treasure Pocket—Accent
Page 119

9d. Treasure Pocket—Folio
Page 119

Sampler™

10a. Sampler—Nine Photo Quilt
Page 122

10b. Sampler—Flower
Page 122

10c. Sampler—Mix
Page 123

10c. Photo Alternate
Page 123

10c. Photo Alternate
Page 123

10d. Sampler—Pieced
Page 124

10e. Sampler—Photo Checkerboard
Page 125

10f. Sampler—Captivating Corners
Page 126

10g. Sampler—Collage
Page 127

10h. Sampler—Calendar
Page 127

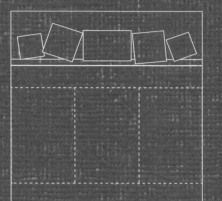

Title Topper™

I have two real, abiding passions: my family and artwork. Scrapbooking celebrates both—capturing the sweet relationships I share with my four children, who are growing into smart, unique, individuals; and preserving our memories together in simply beautiful artwork that will last through generations.

This layout proclaims my heart: My children are my world. Let the world know what your layouts mean to you when you use Title Topper patterns, designed to bring your title to the fore, sweetly singing the praises of the photos in your artwork.

Title Topper–Subtle™

Paper Dimensions

A 8" × 12"

B 6" × 12"

C 1" × 12"

D 3" × 11" (vellum)

Assembly Instructions

1. Using one 12" × 12" cardstock as your base, attach piece A to the bottom of the page, keeping the edges flush.

2. Attach piece B, placing it 1" from the top of piece A, keeping the side edges flush.

3. Attach piece C directly above piece A, keeping the edges flush.

4. Attach piece D, placing it ½" from the top and side edges.

5. Attach photos, title, and journaling as desired.

Companion Layouts

2c, 2f, 2g, 2k, 3a, 3b, 3f, 4d, 4l, 4m, 5b, 6d, 6h, 7f, 7g, 7j, 8e, 8g, 8h, 9a, 9b, 10c

COVER CHIPBOARD SHAPES WITH PATTERNED PAPER

Add texture, interest, and fun to your projects by covering chipboard shapes with patterned paper before you attach them to your pages. Choose colors and designs that complement the layout and you'll have an eye-catching element that livens up your artwork!

Master Pattern

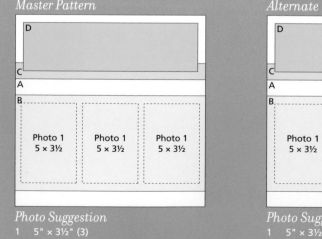

D

C

A

B

| Photo 1 5 × 3½ | Photo 1 5 × 3½ | Photo 1 5 × 3½ |

Photo Suggestion

1 5" × 3½" (3)

Alternate

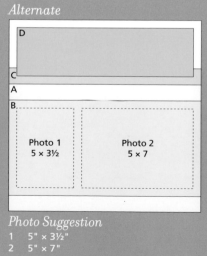

D

C

A

B

| Photo 1 5 × 3½ | Photo 2 5 × 7 |

Photo Suggestion

1 5" × 3½"

2 5" × 7"

Alternate

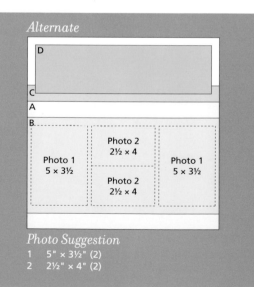

D

C

A

B

| Photo 1 5 × 3½ | Photo 2 2½ × 4 / Photo 2 2½ × 4 | Photo 1 5 × 3½ |

Photo Suggestion

1 5" × 3½" (2)

2 2½" × 4" (2)

Title Topper–Billboard™

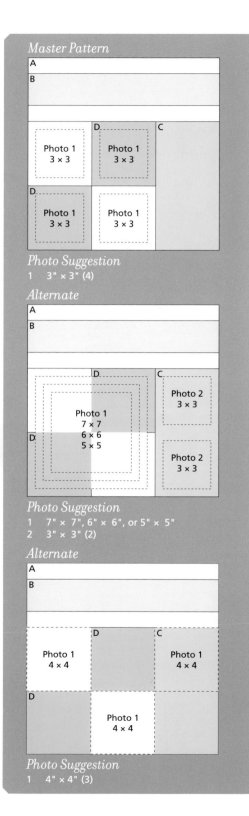

Paper Dimensions

A 4" × 12"

B 2" × 12"

C 8" × 4"

D 4" × 4" (2)

Companion Layouts

2c, 2f, 2g, 2i, 3d, 3f, 3h, 4a, 4d, 5f, 6c, 8h, 9a, 10a

HIDE-AND-SEEK JOURNALING

It's great fun to use photos as pockets to "hide" your journaling on a layout. Simply adhere three edges of the photo(s) to the page, then slip a journaling strip behind the photo. Kids of all ages will love it!

Assembly Instructions

1. Using one 12" × 12" cardstock as your base, attach piece A to the top of the page, keeping the edges flush.

2. Attach piece B to piece A, placing it 1" from the top, keeping the side edges flush.

3. Attach piece C to the bottom right corner of the page, keeping the edges flush.

4. Attach one piece D to the bottom left corner of the page, keeping the edges flush. Attach remaining piece D directly under piece A and directly to the left of piece C, keeping the edges flush.

5. Attach photos, title, and journaling as desired.

Title Topper—Pieced Together™

READY-MADE PHOTO FRAMES

Use the versatile metal-rimmed tag as a stunning photo frame! Just trim the photo to match the shape and size of the tag, then adhere it to the white paper inside the tag. These small gems can be placed anywhere on a layout to add eye-catching interest and dimension.

Paper Dimensions

A   3" × 1½" (3)

B   3" × 1½" (3)

C   7" × 11"

D   6" × 10"

Assembly Instructions

1. Using one 12" × 12" cardstock as your base, arrange and attach pieces A and B across the top of the page, centering them from side to side and alternating placement between ½" and 1" from the top.

2. Attach piece C, placing it ½" from the bottom and side edges of the page.

3. Attach piece D to the center of piece C.

4. Attach photos, title, and journaling as desired.

Companion Layouts

1c (rotated),2b, 2f, 2g, 2i, 2j, 3a, 3b, 3d, 3f, 3h, 3i, 3j, 4a, 5f, 5h, 6a, 6c, 6f, 6i, 7c, 7f, 7g, 8c, 8f, 8g, 8j, 9a

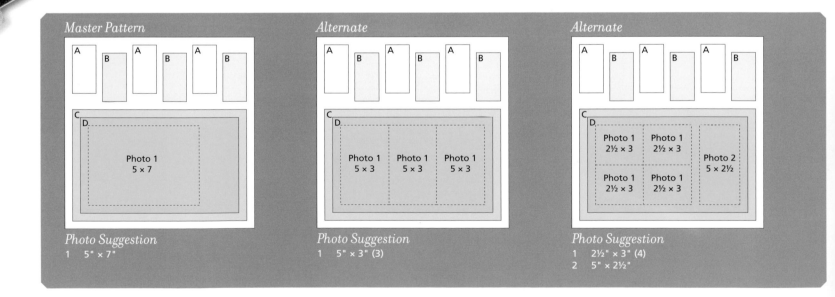

Master Pattern

Photo 1
5 × 7

Photo Suggestion
1   5" × 7"

Alternate

Photo 1
5 × 3   Photo 1
5 × 3   Photo 1
5 × 3

Photo Suggestion
1   5" × 3" (3)

Alternate

Photo 1
2½ × 3   Photo 1
2½ × 3   Photo 2
5 × 2½

Photo 1
2½ × 3   Photo 1
2½ × 3

Photo Suggestion
1   2½" × 3" (4)
2   5" × 2½"

Title Topper™

Title Topper–Heading™

Paper Dimensions

A   11" × 11"

B   3" × 12"

Assembly Instructions

1. Using one 12" × 12" cardstock as your base, attach piece A to the center of the page.

2. Attach piece B, placing it 1" from the top of the page, keeping the side edges flush.

3. Attach photos, title, and journaling as desired.

Companion Layouts

2b, 2e, 2f, 2g, 2i, 2l, 3a, 3b, 3d, 3e, 3f, 3g, 4a, 4e, 4l, 5g, 6c, 6g, 7c, 7g, 7h, 8a, 8f, 8h, 9a, 10a, 10e, 10g

CAPTIVATING CARDSTOCK PHOTO BORDERS

For a distinctive look, fold colored cardstock strips in half and slip them beneath a photo's edges to create a fashionable border. Using different sizes and colors, you can complement any layout for an outstanding effect.

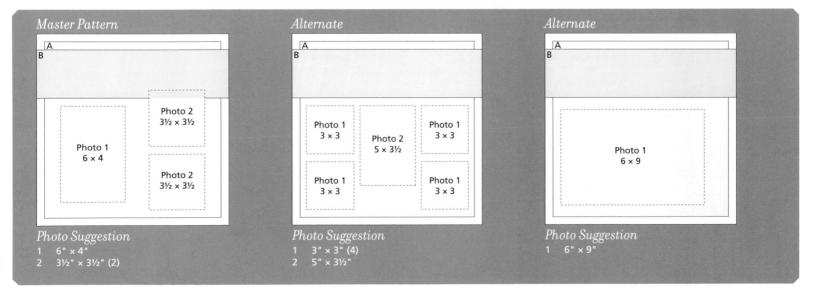

Master Pattern

Photo 1
6 × 4

Photo 2
3½ × 3½

Photo 2
3½ × 3½

Photo Suggestion
1   6" × 4"
2   3½" × 3½" (2)

Alternate

Photo 1
3 × 3

Photo 2
5 × 3½

Photo 1
3 × 3

Photo 1
3 × 3

Photo 1
3 × 3

Photo Suggestion
1   3" × 3" (4)
2   5" × 3½"

Alternate

Photo 1
6 × 9

Photo Suggestion
1   6" × 9"

Title Topper—Equal Portions™

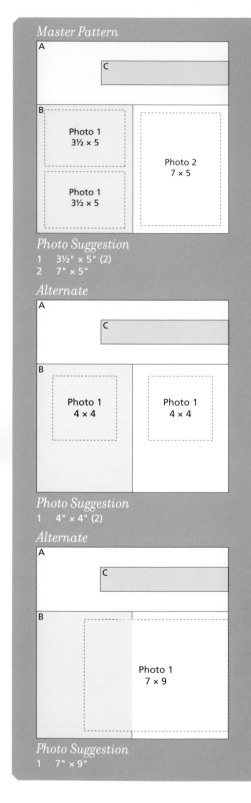

Master Pattern

A	
	C

B	
Photo 1 3½ × 5	Photo 2 7 × 5
Photo 1 3½ × 5	

Photo Suggestion
1   3½" × 5" (2)
2   7" × 5"

Alternate

A	
	C

B	
Photo 1 4 × 4	Photo 1 4 × 4

Photo Suggestion
1   4" × 4" (2)

Alternate

A	
	C

B	
	Photo 1 7 × 9

Photo Suggestion
1   7" × 9"

Paper Dimensions

A   4" × 12"

B   8" × 6"

C   1½" × 8"

LOVE BLOOMS

Paper flowers are perfect for creating an adorable "love me, love me not" look. Fold flowers in half and adhere them as desired to the layout, then place several single petals randomly on the page for a romantic ambience.

Assembly Instructions

1. Using one 12" × 12" cardstock as your base, attach piece A to the top of the page, keeping the edges flush.

2. Attach piece B to the bottom left corner of the page, keeping the edges flush.

3. Attach piece C to piece A, placing it 1" from the top, keeping the right edges flush.

4. Attach photos, title, and journaling as desired.

Companion Layouts

1e (rotated), 2b, 2e, 2f, 2g, 2h, 2j, 3a, 3b, 3f, 3h, 4b, 4c, 4d, 5b, 5l, 6d, 6g, 6h, 7c, 7f, 8b, 8f, 8g, 9a, 9b, 9d

Title Topper—Center Focus™

Paper Dimensions

A   2½" × 12"

B   8" × 5"

Assembly Instructions

1. Using one 12" × 12" cardstock as your base, attach piece A, placing it 1½" from the top of the page, keeping the side edges flush.

2. Attach piece B to the bottom of the page directly under piece A, centering it 3½" from the sides.

3. Attach photos, title, and journaling as desired.

Companion Layouts

2e, 2g, 2h, 2i, 3a, 3b, 3c, 3f, 6f, 6i, 7f, 7j, 8e, 8g, 8h

FAUX PHOTO FILTER

Add mystery and intrigue to your layout by creating the illusion of a filtered photo. Simply swipe the edges of a photo across an ink pad, and the result will be a lovely blurring effect. Perfect for family, travel, outdoor photos and more!

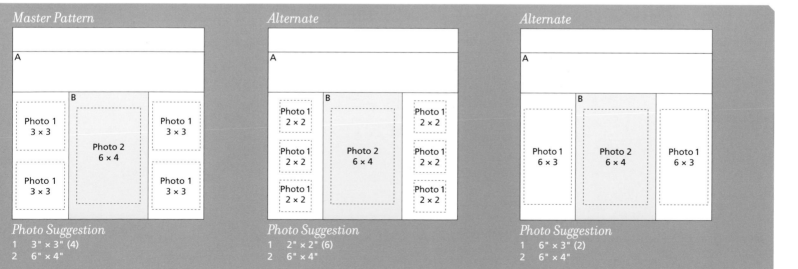

Master Pattern

A

B

| Photo 1 3 × 3 | Photo 2 6 × 4 | Photo 1 3 × 3 |
| Photo 1 3 × 3 | | Photo 1 3 × 3 |

Photo Suggestion
1   3" × 3" (4)
2   6" × 4"

Alternate

A

B

Photo 1 2 × 2	Photo 2 6 × 4	Photo 1 2 × 2
Photo 1 2 × 2		Photo 1 2 × 2
Photo 1 2 × 2		Photo 1 2 × 2

Photo Suggestion
1   2" × 2" (6)
2   6" × 4"

Alternate

A

B

| Photo 1 6 × 3 | Photo 2 6 × 4 | Photo 1 6 × 3 |

Photo Suggestion
1   6" × 3" (2)
2   6" × 4"

Title Topper–Add Up™

Paper Dimensions

A   8½" × 12"

B   6" × 12"

C   ½" × 12"

D   Various Sizes

Assembly Instructions

1. Using one 12" × 12" cardstock as your base, attach piece A to the bottom of the page, keeping the edges flush.

2. Attach piece B, to the center of piece A, keeping the side edges flush.

3. Attach piece C directly above piece A, keeping the edges flush.

4. Attach pieces D as desired across the top of piece C.

5. Attach photos, title, and journaling as desired.

Companion Layouts

1g (rotated), 2b, 2e, 2g, 2k, 3b, 3h, 4d, 4h, 4k, 4l, 5f, 6b, 6c, 6d, 6e, 6f, 8a, 8c, 8e, 8h

SPRUCE UP PRINTED STITCHES

Add dimension, texture, and fun to printed stitches by hand stitching on top of the printing with a coordinating fiber of your choice.

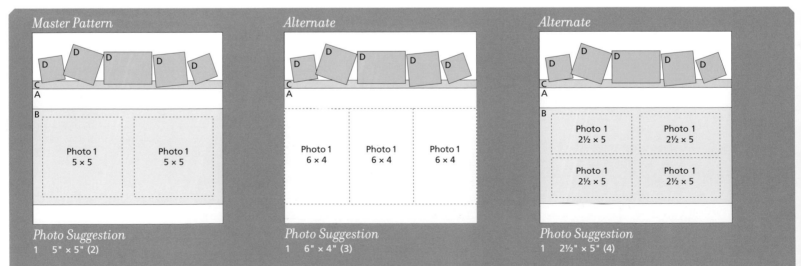

Master Pattern

Photo 1
5 × 5

Photo 1
5 × 5

Photo Suggestion

1   5" × 5" (2)

Alternate

Photo 1
6 × 4

Photo 1
6 × 4

Photo 1
6 × 4

Photo Suggestion

1   6" × 4" (3)

Alternate

Photo 1
2½ × 5

Photo 1
2½ × 5

Photo 1
2½ × 5

Photo 1
2½ × 5

Photo Suggestion

1   2½" × 5" (4)

Title Topper—Photos™

Paper Dimensions

A 6" × 12"

B 5" × 12"

C 5½" × 5"

Assembly Instructions

1. Using one 12" × 12" cardstock as your base, attach piece A, placing it ½" from the top, keeping the side edges flush.

2. Attach piece B to the center of piece A, keeping the side edges flush.

3. Attach piece C to the bottom left corner of the page, keeping the edges flush.

4. Attach photos, title, and journaling as desired.

Companion Layouts

1h (rotated), 2c, 2f, 3a, 3f, 4h, 6d, 7c

EMBOSSING A TITLE

When embossing, if an area does not cover completely, rather than starting over just fill in the spaces with a coordinating marker.

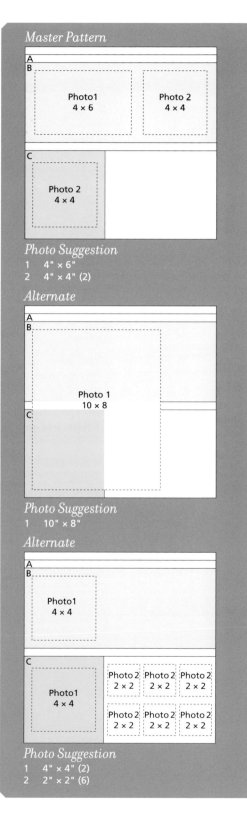

Master Pattern

A
B

Photo1
4 × 6

Photo 2
4 × 4

C

Photo 2
4 × 4

Photo Suggestion
1   4" × 6"
2   4" × 4" (2)

Alternate

A
B

Photo 1
10 × 8

C

Photo Suggestion
1   10" × 8"

Alternate

A
B

Photo1
4 × 4

C

Photo1
4 × 4

Photo 2
2 × 2

Photo 2
2 × 2

Photo 2
2 × 2

Photo 2
2 × 2

Photo 2
2 × 2

Photo 2
2 × 2

Photo Suggestion
1   4" × 4" (2)
2   2" × 2" (6)

1i • *Title Topper–Basic*™

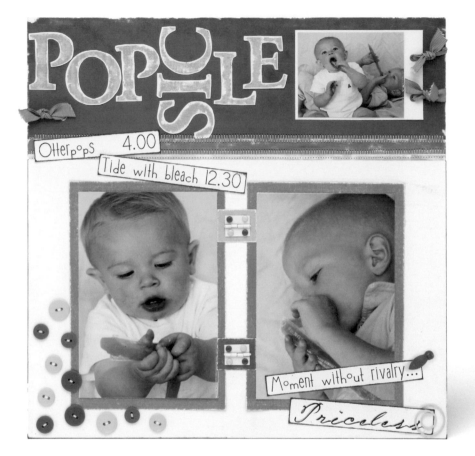

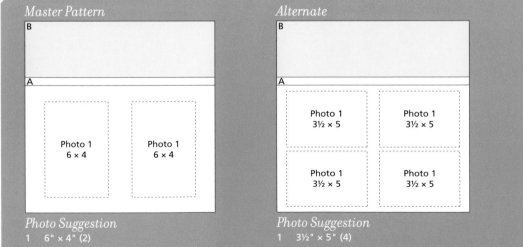

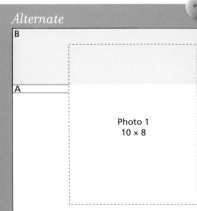

Paper Dimensions

A   4" × 12"

B   3½" × 12"

Assembly Instructions

1. Using one 12" × 12" cardstock as your base, attach piece A to the top of the page, keeping the edges flush.

2. Attach piece B to the top of piece A, keeping the edges flush.

3. Attach photos, title, and journaling as desired.

Companion Layouts

1i (rotated), 2b, 2e, 2f, 2g, 2j, 2k, 3a, 3b, 3f, 4b, 4d, 4e, 7f, 8a, 8b, 8f, 8h, 9a, 10d, 10h

CLUSTERING BUTTONS

Spark instant interest in your layout by clustering different sizes, shapes, and colors of buttons on the page. Don't overdo it, but one or two clusters strategically glued or stitched on a page will really make your artwork pop.

Master Pattern

B
A

Photo 1
6 × 4

Photo 1
6 × 4

Photo Suggestion
1   6" × 4" (2)

Alternate

B
A

Photo 1
3½ × 5

Photo 1
3½ × 5

Photo 1
3½ × 5

Photo 1
3½ × 5

Photo Suggestion
1   3½" × 5" (4)

Alternate

B
A

Photo 1
10 × 8

Photo Suggestion
1   10" × 8"

Title Topper–Cover™

Paper Dimensions

A   8½" × 12"

B   2" × 12"

Assembly Instructions

1. Using one 12" × 12" cardstock as your base, attach piece A to the bottom of the page, keeping the edges flush.

2. Attach piece B directly above piece A, keeping the edges flush.

3. Attach photos, title, and journaling as desired.

Companion Layouts

1j (rotated), 2b, 2e, 2g, 2i, 2l, 3a, 3b, 4a, 4k, 4l, 6c, 6d, 8a, 9a

TEARING DECORATIVE BORDERS

Artfully torn paper—using either solid cardstock or patterned papers—can be a wonderful way to add interest, texture, and dimension to your layout. Tear the paper on one side to fashion a border or to frame photos and embellishments.

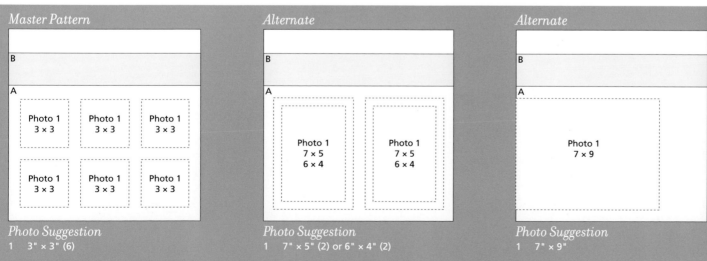

Master Pattern

B

A

| Photo 1 3 × 3 | Photo 1 3 × 3 | Photo 1 3 × 3 |
| Photo 1 3 × 3 | Photo 1 3 × 3 | Photo 1 3 × 3 |

Photo Suggestion
1   3" × 3" (6)

Alternate

B

A

| Photo 1 7 × 5 6 × 4 | Photo 1 7 × 5 6 × 4 |

Photo Suggestion
1   7" × 5" (2) or 6" × 4" (2)

Alternate

B

A

Photo 1 7 × 9

Photo Suggestion
1   7" × 9"

Bottom Border™

Transitions: proof that time goes by and the world goes on. Watching my son marry his sweetheart was the happiest of transitions. It meant letting go of my little boy . . . but also welcoming a beautiful new daughter to my family.

This Bottom Border pattern uses an eye-catching sequence of photos perfect for catching the transitions of your life. In many ways, scrapbooking helps us let go—and hold on—no matter what changes we encounter.

The world
goes on
all around
but for
two happy
people,
*time
stands
still*

Bottom Border–Four in a Row™

Paper Dimensions

A   11" × 11"

B   6" × 8"

C   3½" × 12"

Assembly Instructions

1. Using one 12" × 12" cardstock as your base, attach piece A to the center of the page.

2. Attach piece B to the left side of the page, placing it 1" from the top, keeping the left edges flush.

3. Attach piece C, placing it 1" from the bottom, keeping the side edges flush.

4. Attach photos, title, and journaling as desired.

Companion Layouts

2a, 3b, 3f, 3j, 6c, 8c

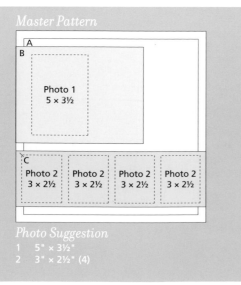
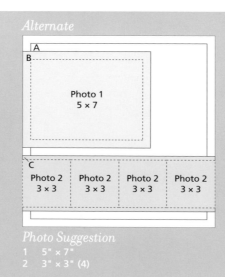
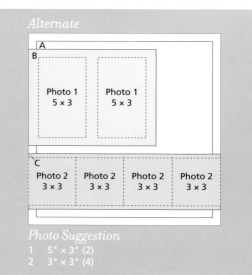

OFFSET STITCHING

When you're doing diagonal hand stitching on a layout, here's a great tip to keep the stitching uniform. Using a piercing tool, poke one row of holes; then poke another row of holes just above and to the right. With the holes offset in this manner, when you stitch between the rows, the stitching will be diagonal instead of straight up-and-down.

Master Pattern

A	
B	

Photo 1
5 × 3½

C

| Photo 2 3 × 2½ | Photo 2 3 × 2½ | Photo 2 3 × 2½ | Photo 2 3 × 2½ |

Photo Suggestion
1   5" × 3½"
2   3" × 2½" (4)

Alternate

A	
B	

Photo 1
5 × 7

C

| Photo 2 3 × 3 | Photo 2 3 × 3 | Photo 2 3 × 3 | Photo 2 3 × 3 |

Photo Suggestion
1   5" × 7"
2   3" × 3" (4)

Alternate

A	
B	

| Photo 1 5 × 3 | Photo 1 5 × 3 |

C

| Photo 2 3 × 3 | Photo 2 3 × 3 | Photo 2 3 × 3 | Photo 2 3 × 3 |

Photo Suggestion
1   5" × 3" (2)
2   3" × 3" (4)

© 2007 JRL Publications

Bottom Border–Diagonal Accent™

FAUX DENIM

To create a delightful denim look on all or part of your layout, attach a sheet of adhesive-backed twill to your basic cardstock, then apply a combination of dark and medium blue ink to all or sections of the sheet. The unique weave of the twill creates an appearance of denim—great for an outdoors or sporty layout!

Master Pattern

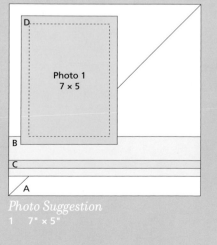

```
D
      Photo 1
       7 × 5
B
C
  A
```

Photo Suggestion

1   7" × 5"

Paper Dimensions

A   12" × 12" (torn diagonally)

B   2½" × 12"

C   ½" × 12"

D   8" × 6"

Companion Layouts

1d, 1e, 1j, 3b, 3h, 5b, 5g, 5l, 6e, 6h, 6i, 7j, 8a, 8b, 8c, 8d, 8f, 8g, 8h, 8j, 9c, 10c

Assembly Instructions

1. Decoratively tear or cut piece A in half diagonally. Using one 12" × 12" cardstock as your base, attach piece A to the bottom right corner of the page.

2. Attach piece B, placing it 1¼" from the bottom, keeping the side edges flush.

3. Attach piece C, placing it ½" from the bottom of piece B, keeping the side edges flush.

4. Attach piece D, placing it ¾" from the top and left edges of the page.

5. Attach photos, title, and journaling as desired.

Bottom Border–Portrait™

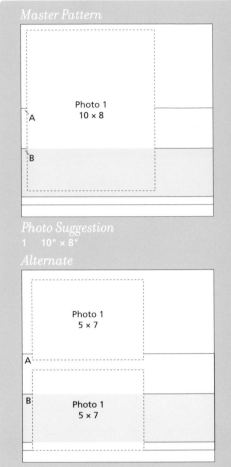

Photo Suggestion
1   10" × 8"

Alternate

Photo Suggestion
1   5" × 7" (2)

Paper Dimensions

A   6" × 12"

B   3" × 12"

Assembly Instructions

1. Using one 12" × 12" cardstock as your base, attach piece A, placing it ¾" from the bottom, keeping the side edges flush.

2. Attach piece B, placing it ½" from the bottom of piece A, keeping the side edges flush.

3. Attach photos, title, and journaling as desired.

Companion Layouts

1a, 1d, 1h, 1i, 2g, 2i, 2k, 3a, 3b, 3f, 3h, 4e, 5a, 5d, 5h, 6b, 6f, 6h, 6i, 7c, 7d, 7e, 7f, 7h, 8a, 8b, 8c, 8d, 8f, 8g, 8h, 9a, 9c, 10d

SOFTEN COLORS WITH VELLUM

You can mute and soften the color of any cardstock or patterned paper by simply applying vellum over it. Make the page even more interesting and diverse by applying the vellum only to selected areas of the page, thus making some parts brighter and others more subdued.

Bottom Border–Base™

Paper Dimensions

A	12" × 12"
B	4" × 12"
C	3½" × 12"
D	8" × 8½"
E	3½" × 3½"

Assembly Instructions

1. Using one 12" × 12" cardstock as your base, attach piece A, adhering all sides except the top left corner of the page.

2. Attach piece B, placing it ½" from the bottom of the page, keeping the side edges flush.

3. Attach piece C to the center of piece B, keeping the side edges flush.

4. Attach piece D, placing it ½" from the top and right edges of the page.

5. Attach piece E to the back side of the top left corner of piece A. Fold back the corner 3" to show the contrasting piece E.

6. Attach photos, title, and journaling as desired.

Companion Layouts

1e, 3b, 3f, 6h, 6i, 8b, 8j, 10c

ACCENT WITH BRADS

Brads can be used too adorn your page as a fun design element, but keep in mind they are practical too. Use brads to hold open folded corners, to attach vellum without adhesive, or to hold journaling in place. Brads are a simple accent, but always add that perfect finishing touch.

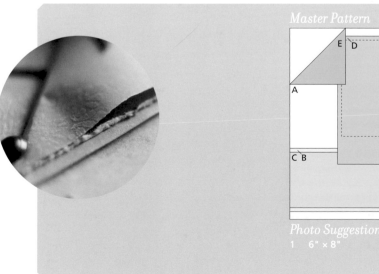

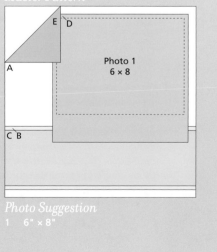

Master Pattern

E D

A

Photo 1
6 × 8

C B

Photo Suggestion
1   6" × 8"

Bottom Border–Tucked In™

Paper Dimensions

A 5" × 12"

B 2" × 12"

C 6" × 8"

Assembly Instructions

1. Using one 12" × 12" cardstock as your base, attach piece A to the bottom of the page, keeping the edges flush, adhering only the bottom and side edges in order to form a pocket.

2. Attach piece B to the center of piece A, keeping the side edges flush.

3. Attach piece C, tucking it behind piece A, placing it 1¾" from the top and 2" from the sides of the page.

4. Attach photos, title, and journaling as desired.

Companion Layouts

1d, 1e, 1i, 3a, 3b, 3f, 3h, 5c, 6e, 7e, 7f, 7j, 8b, 8g, 8j

Charlotte
Summer
2006

LOVED
you are

Master Pattern

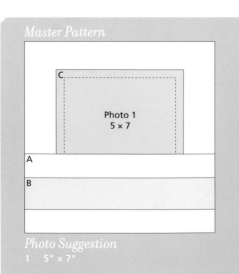

C

Photo 1
5 × 7

A

B

Photo Suggestion
1   5" × 7"

Alternate

C

Photo 1
5 × 3½

Photo 1
5 × 3½

A

B

Photo Suggestion
1   5" × 3½" (2)

ARTISTIC TITLES

Using an artistic element for your title adds a distinctive and classy touch to any project. You can use one made of chipboard, fabric, stickers, or even brads. Use your imagination, and you'll come up with the perfect combination!

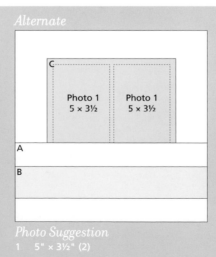

Bottom Border–Footnotes™

Paper Dimensions

A   4" × 12"

B   2" × 12"

C   2½" × 8"

D   6" × 8"

PHOTO CRUMPLING

A photo will really pop on a page if its texture is changed a bit. Dampen and crumple your photo as much as desired, then let it dry and iron it gently to smooth it out a bit. Attached to the layout, it becomes an attractive focal point.

Assembly Instructions

1. Using one 12" × 12" cardstock as your base, attach piece A, placing it 1" from the bottom, keeping the side edges flush.

2. Attach piece B to the center of piece A, keeping the side edges flush.

3. Attach piece C, placing it ¾" from the bottom and ½" from the right edge of piece A.

4. Attach piece D, placing ½" from the top and right edges of the page.

Companion Layouts

1b, 1c, 1d, 1e, 1h, 1i, 1j, 3b, 3f, 3h, 3i, 6b, 6h, 7e, 8b, 10c

Master Pattern

D

Photo 1
5 × 7

A

B   C

Photo Suggestion

1   5" × 7"

Alternate

D

Photo 1
5 × 3½   Photo 1
5 × 3½

A

B   C

Photo Suggestion

1   5" × 3½" (2)

Ellie
Florida
2006

I adore this picture of you. This is your "signature face of mischief". I snapped this photo when I caught you burying your sister's flip flops in the sand. I love the sneaky side of you and I hope you never change.

Bottom Border—Quartet™

Paper Dimensions

A   5" × 12"

Assembly Instructions

1. Using one 12" × 12" cardstock as your base, attach piece A, placing it ½" from the bottom of the page, keeping the side edges flush.

2. Attach photos, title, and journaling as desired.

Companion Layouts

1d, 3i, 5d, 9b, 10c

TYING IT ALL TOGETHER

To achieve a wonderfully coordinated look, match the color of the fibers in the buttons on your page with the color of ink used to distress the edges of the page. It seems like a small thing—but this technique makes any layout especially easy on the eye!

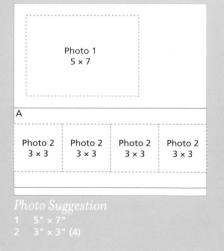

Master Pattern

Photo 1 5½ × 3½	Photo 1 5½ × 3½

A

Photo 2 3 × 3	Photo 2 3 × 3	Photo 2 3 × 3	Photo 2 3 × 3

Photo Suggestion
1   5½" × 3½" (2)
2   3" × 3" (4)

Alternate

Photo 1 5 × 7

A

Photo 2 3 × 3	Photo 2 3 × 3	Photo 2 3 × 3	Photo 2 3 × 3

Photo Suggestion
1   5" × 7"
2   3" × 3" (4)

Bottom Border–Triple Combination™

Paper Dimensions

A   2" × 12"

B   3" × 3" (2)

C   4" × 4"

Assembly Instructions

1. Using one 12" × 12" cardstock as your base, attach piece A, placing it 1½" from the bottom of the page keeping the side edges flush.

2. Attach one piece B, placing it ½" from the left and 1" from the bottom of the page. Attach remaining piece B, placing it ½" from the right and 1" from the bottom of the page.

3. Attach piece C centered between both pieces B, and ½" from the bottom of the page.

4. Attach photos, title, and journaling as desired.

Companion Layouts

1b, 2i, 3b, 3f, 3h, 5h, 7j, 10a

A SIMPLE SOLUTION

Sometimes you'll have several great photos to use in a layout, but the colors don't really coordinate. Not to worry—simply use your computer photo editing program to change the pictures to black and white (or, if you don't have digital photos, use a copying machine to make black and white reproductions).

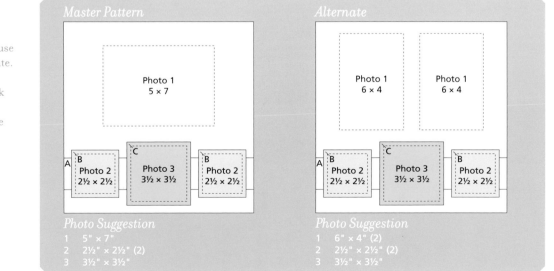

Master Pattern

Photo 1
5 × 7

A   B   Photo 2   2½ × 2½   C   Photo 3   3½ × 3½   B   Photo 2   2½ × 2½

Photo Suggestion
1   5" × 7"
2   2½" × 2½" (2)
3   3½" × 3½"

Alternate

Photo 1
6 × 4   Photo 1
6 × 4

A   B   Photo 2   2½ × 2½   C   Photo 3   3½ × 3½   B   Photo 2   2½ × 2½

Photo Suggestion
1   6" × 4" (2)
2   2½" × 2½" (2)
3   3½" × 3½"

2i • Bottom Border–Overlap™

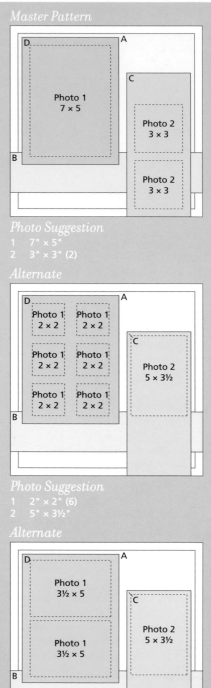

Master Pattern

D | A
Photo 1
7 × 5
C
Photo 2
3 × 3
B
Photo 2
3 × 3

Photo Suggestion
1 7" × 5"
2 3" × 3" (2)

Alternate

D | A
Photo 1
2 × 2 | Photo 1
2 × 2
Photo 1
2 × 2 | Photo 1
2 × 2
C
Photo 2
5 × 3½
Photo 1
2 × 2 | Photo 1
2 × 2
B

Photo Suggestion
1 2" × 2" (6)
2 5" × 3½"

Alternate

D | A
Photo 1
3½ × 5
C
Photo 2
5 × 3½
Photo 1
3½ × 5
B

Photo Suggestion
1 3½" × 5" (2)
2 5" × 3½"

Paper Dimensions

A   11" × 11"

B   2½" × 12"

C   9" × 4"

D   8" × 6"

Assembly Instructions

1. Using one 12" × 12" cardstock as your base, attach piece A to the center of the page.

2. Attach piece B, placing it 1½" from the bottom of the page, keeping the side edges flush.

3. Attach piece C to the bottom of the page, placing it ¾" from the right edge of the page, keeping the bottom edges flush.

4. Attach piece D, placing it ¾" from the top and left edges of the page.

5. Attach photos, title, and journaling as desired.

Companion Layouts

1b, 1c, 1d, 1j, 3i, 3j, 7g, 7j, 9a, 10a

NOW YOU SEE IT...

Need a convenient place to "hide" your journaling? Try cutting a slit all the way through the cardstock to the back of the layout, then inserting a journaling strip. Your page protector will hold it in place on the opposite side of the page, and you can easily access the strip from the front.

Bottom Border–Title™

Paper Dimensions

A 2½" × 12"

B 9" × 6"

C 7" × 12"

D 5" × 12"

Assembly Instructions

1. Using one 12" × 12" cardstock as your base, attach piece A, placing it ½" from the bottom of the page, keeping the side edges flush.

2. Attach piece B to the right side of the page, placing it 1" from the top, keeping the right edges flush.

3. Attach piece C, placing it 1½" from the top of the page, keeping the side edges flush.

4. Attach piece D to the center of piece C, keeping the side edges flush.

5. Attach photos, title, and journaling as desired.

Companion Layouts

3b, 3f, 4a, 4d, 5d, 6d, 6h, 7e, 8g, 9a, 9b

UNDERLINING WITH HEMP

A few thick stitches of hemp below a title will really make it stand out on the page as the focal point of your layout. Fabulous fibers are a cinch to add interest and great texture!

Master Pattern

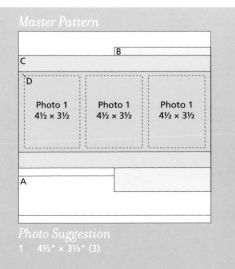

Photo 1 4½ × 3½	Photo 1 4½ × 3½	Photo 1 4½ × 3½

Photo Suggestion
1 4½" × 3½" (3)

Alternate

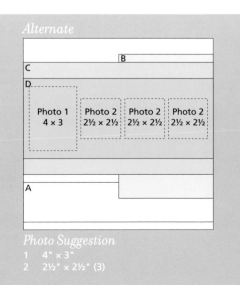

Photo 1 4 × 3 | Photo 2 2½ × 2½ | Photo 2 2½ × 2½ | Photo 2 2½ × 2½

Photo Suggestion
1 4" × 3"
2 2½" × 2½" (3)

Alternate

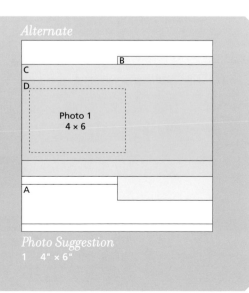

Photo 1 4 × 6

Photo Suggestion
1 4" × 6"

2k • *Bottom Border–Photo Focus*™

Paper Dimensions

A   10" × 12"

B   9½" × 12"

Assembly Instructions

1. Using one 12" × 12" cardstock as your base, attach piece A to the top of the page, keeping the top and side edges flush.

2. Attach piece B to the top of piece A, keeping the top and side edges flush.

3. Attach photos, title, and journaling as desired.

Companion Layouts

3a, 3d, 4f, 4h, 4l, 4m, 4n, 5a, 5k, 6b, 6c

CREATING BUTTONS

It's easy to make your own decorative buttons using chipboard, cardstock, and clear liquid glaze. Choose chipboard of desired shapes and sizes, then cover the pieces with cardstock of your choice. Use a piercing tool to make button holes in each piece and attach them to the layout with fiber or thread. Cover each button with clear liquid glaze and allow to dry. These will really pop on the layout!

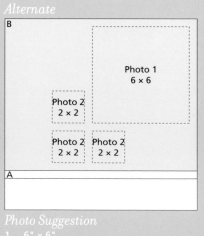

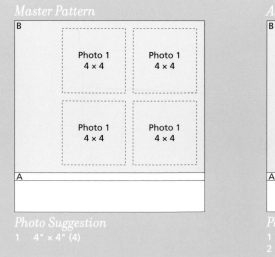

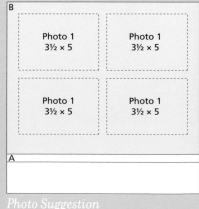

Master Pattern

Photo 1 4 × 4	Photo 1 4 × 4
Photo 1 4 × 4	Photo 1 4 × 4

B / **A**

Photo Suggestion
1   4" × 4" (4)

Alternate

	Photo 1 6 × 6
Photo 2 2 × 2	
Photo 2 2 × 2	Photo 2 2 × 2

B / **A**

Photo Suggestion
1   6" × 6"
2   2" × 2" (3)

Alternate

Photo 1 3½ × 5	Photo 1 3½ × 5
Photo 1 3½ × 5	Photo 1 3½ × 5

B / **A**

Photo Suggestion
1   3½" × 5" (4)

Bottom Border–Layered™

Paper Dimensions

A   4" × 12"

B   3" × 12"

C   1½" × 12"

D   ½" × 12"

Assembly Instructions

1. Using one 12" × 12" cardstock as your base, attach piece A, placing it ¼" from the bottom of the page, keeping the side edges flush.

2. Attach piece B to the center of piece A, keeping the side edges flush.

3. Attach piece C, placing it ½" from the bottom of piece B, keeping the side edges flush.

4. Attach piece D, placing ¼" from the bottom of piece C, keeping the side edges flush.

5. Attach photos, title, and journaling as desired.

Companion Layouts

2k, 3f, 3h, 5l, 7h, 8b, 9d, 10a

CLEVER STOWAWAYS

Conceal photos or journaling and achieve great dimension at the same time! Place 3-D foam squares along the back of three sides of your photos and attach them to the layout. Then slide additional photos or journaling inside the pockets—a slick way to make more space for treasured memories!

Master Pattern

Photo 1
6 × 6

A
B
C
D

Photo Suggestion

1   6" × 6"

Alternate

Photo 1
5 × 4

Photo 1
5 × 4

Photo 1
5 × 4

A
B
C
D

Photo Suggestion

1   5" × 4" (3)

Alternate

Photo 1
7 × 5

Photo 1
7 × 5

A
B
C
D

Photo Suggestion

1   7" × 5" (2)

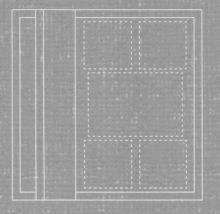

Sidebar™

My life with David has been a walk on the wild side! Funny, compassionate, and an active, adoring dad, my husband has taught me that life is more fun when it's accented with adventure.

Too, scrapbooking is more fun when accented with embellishments that bring out the creative creature in you. It only takes minutes to transform a simple pattern like this Sidebar into a showpiece with dimension and drama—roaring with metal accents, stitchery, even a 3-D title. Try all the techniques in *Reflections*™ to set your imagination loose!

Our trip to the

Sidebar–Original™

Paper Dimensions

A   12" × 4"

B   12" × ½"

C   3½" × 3½"

D   10" × 7"

Assembly Instructions

1. Using one 12" × 12" cardstock as your base, attach piece A to the left side of the page, keeping the edges flush.

2. Attach piece B to the right side of piece A, keeping the edges flush.

3. Attach piece C, placing it 1" from the bottom and ¼" from the left side of the page.

4. Attach piece D, placing it 1" from the top and ½" from the right edge of the page.

5. Attach photos, title, and journaling as desired.

Companion Layouts

1d, 1f, 1i, 1j, 2b, 2g, 2j, 3b, 3f, 5h, 8g, 9a, 10a

AGING TAGS WITH RE-INKER

Here's a great way to add an aged look to tags. Place 4–5 drops of re-inker in a small zip-close plastic bag. Dye the tags one at a time by putting them in the bag and squeezing. Add more re-inker as needed.

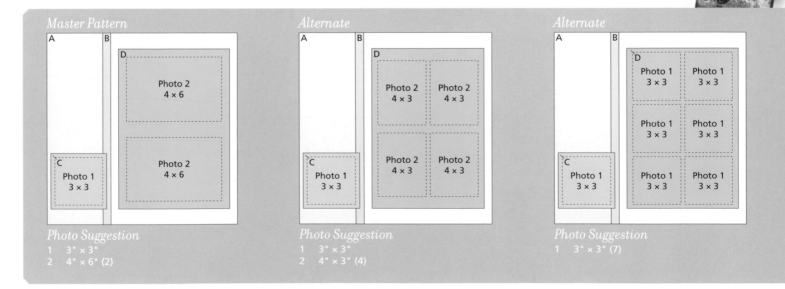

Master Pattern

Photo Suggestion
1   3" × 3"
2   4" × 6" (2)

Alternate

Photo Suggestion
1   3" × 3"
2   4" × 3" (4)

Alternate

Photo Suggestion
1   3" × 3" (7)

Sidebar–Main Frame™

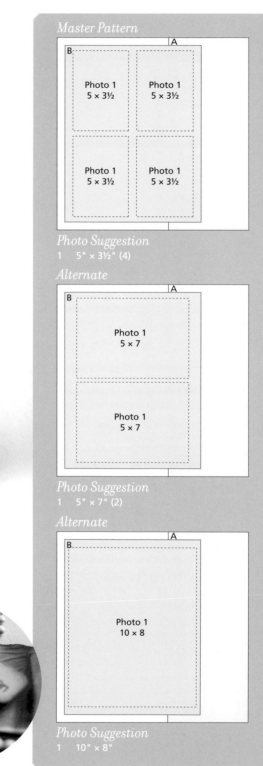

Master Pattern

Photo 1
5 × 3½

Photo 1
5 × 3½

Photo 1
5 × 3½

Photo 1
5 × 3½

Photo Suggestion
1   5" × 3½" (4)

Alternate

Photo 1
5 × 7

Photo 1
5 × 7

Photo Suggestion
1   5" × 7" (2)

Alternate

Photo 1
10 × 8

Photo Suggestion
1   10" × 8"

Paper Dimensions

A   12" × 5"

B   11" × 8½"

Assembly Instructions

1. Using one 12" × 12" cardstock as your base, attach piece A to the right side of the page, keeping the edges flush.

2. Attach piece B, placing it ½" from the top, bottom, and left edges of the page.

3. Attach photos, title, and journaling as desired.

Companion Layouts

3b (rotated)

FUN WITH BRADS

You can do all kinds of creative things with brads. Use them to create letters, whole words, punctuation marks, and eye-catching highlights anywhere on a page. Brads of different colors and sizes add even more interest, and distressing them with sandpaper produces a lovely antiqued look.

Sidebar–Triple™

Master Pattern

A Photo 1 3 × 3

B Photo 1 3 × 3

A Photo 1 3 × 3

C Photo 2 7 × 5

Photo Suggestion

1   3" × 3" (3)
2   7" × 5"

CHIPBOARD BELTS

Use chipboard squares or circles to create sassy belts for fashion pages, accessories for pirate and other adventure layouts, holiday artwork, etc. Shapes can be decorated with paint, stamps, paper, chalks, markers, ribbon, and more.

Paper Dimensions

A   4" × 4" (2)

B   4" × 4"

C   8" × 6"

Companion Layouts

1b, 1d, 1i, 1j, 2i, 3f, 7j, 8h, 10c

Assembly Instructions

1. Using one 12" × 12" cardstock as your base, attach one piece A to the top left corner of the page, keeping the edges flush. Attach remaining piece A to the bottom left corner of the page, keeping the edges flush.

2. Attach piece B between the two pieces A, keeping the edges flush.

3. Attach piece C, placing it 1" from the top and right edges of the page.

4. Attach photos, title, and journaling as desired.

Sidebar–Layers™

STENCIL COLOR TECHNIQUE

Stamp an image on cardstock and cut out, creating a stencil. Stamp the same image on another piece of cardstock and use the stencil to stipple additional color onto the image.

Paper Dimensions

A   4" × 8"

B   12" × 2"

C   12" × 1½"

D   12" × ½"

Assembly Instructions

1. Using one 12" × 12" cardstock as your base, attach piece A to the top left corner of the page, keeping the edges flush.

2. Attach piece B to the right side of the page, keeping the edges flush.

3. Attach piece C directly to the left of piece B, keeping the edges flush.

4. Attach piece D directly to the left of piece C, keeping the edges flush.

5. Attach photos, title, and journaling as desired.

Companion Layouts

3d (rotated)

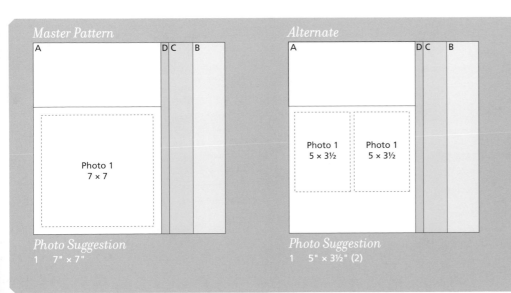

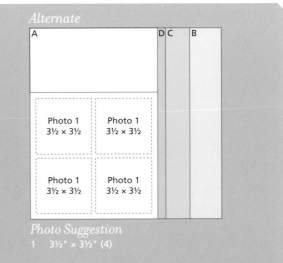

Master Pattern

A | D C | B

Photo 1
7 × 7

Photo Suggestion
1   7" × 7"

Alternate

A | D C | B

Photo 1
5 × 3½ | Photo 1
5 × 3½

Photo Suggestion
1   5" × 3½" (2)

Alternate

A | D C | B

Photo 1
3½ × 3½ | Photo 1
3½ × 3½

Photo 1
3½ × 3½ | Photo 1
3½ × 3½

Photo Suggestion
1   3½" × 3½" (4)

3e ·

Sidebar–Quartet™

Paper Dimensions

A   12" × 4"

B   8" × 8"

C   ½" × 8"

Assembly Instructions

1. Using one 12" × 12" cardstock as your base, attach piece A to the left side of the page, keeping the edges flush.

2. Attach piece B to the bottom right corner of the page, keeping the edges flush.

3. Attach piece C directly above piece B, keeping the right edges flush.

4. Attach photos, title, and journaling as desired.

Companion Layouts

1e, 1g, 1h, 1i, 2c, 2g, 2k, 4f, 4h, 6h, 7j, 8e, 8f, 9d

SEW FINE!

You can machine stitch over ribbon, bunching as you go, for a deliciously gathered effect.

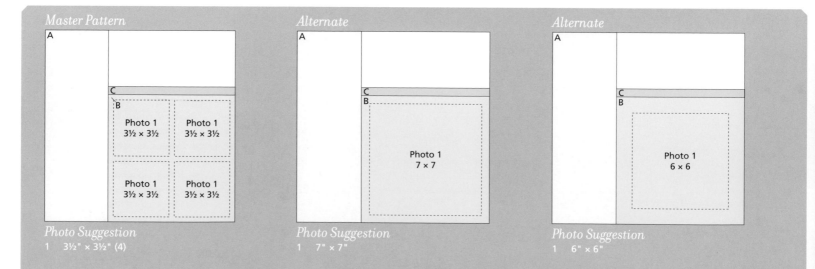

Master Pattern

A

C

B

| Photo 1 3½ × 3½ | Photo 1 3½ × 3½ |
| Photo 1 3½ × 3½ | Photo 1 3½ × 3½ |

Photo Suggestion

1   3½" × 3½" (4)

Alternate

A

C

B

Photo 1
7 × 7

Photo Suggestion

1   7" × 7"

Alternate

A

C

B

Photo 1
6 × 6

Photo Suggestion

1   6" × 6"

Sidebar–Journaling™

Paper Dimensions

A   11" × 8"

B   5" × 7" (2)

C   11" × 2½"

Master Pattern

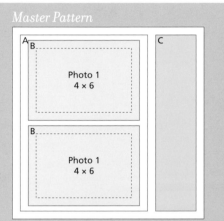

| A | B | | C |

Photo 1
4 × 6

Photo 1
4 × 6

Photo Suggestion

1   4" × 6" (2)

USING CHIPBOARD FRAMES

Use the "skeletons" around chipboard shapes to frame pictures, journaling, and titling, or even accessories you wish to highlight. It's a great way to focus attention on various elements of your layout.

Assembly Instructions

1. Using one 12" × 12" cardstock as your base, attach piece A, placing it ½" from the top, bottom, and left edges of the page.

2. Attach the two pieces B to piece A, placing them ½" from the left and ⅜" from the top and each other.

3. Attach piece C, placing it ½" from the top and right edges of the page.

4. Attach photos, title, and journaling as desired.

Companion Layouts

3f (rotated)

3g • Sidebar—Photo Accent™

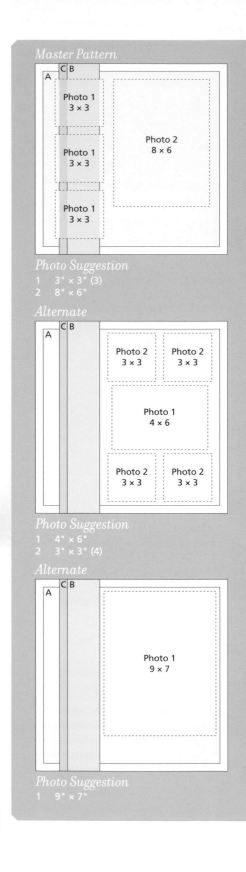

Master Pattern

Photo 1
3 × 3

Photo 1
3 × 3

Photo 1
3 × 3

Photo 2
8 × 6

Photo Suggestion
1   3" × 3" (3)
2   8" × 6"

Alternate

Photo 2
3 × 3

Photo 2
3 × 3

Photo 1
4 × 6

Photo 2
3 × 3

Photo 2
3 × 3

Photo Suggestion
1   4" × 6"
2   3" × 3" (4)

Alternate

Photo 1
9 × 7

Photo Suggestion
1   9" × 7"

Paper Dimensions

A   11" × 11"

B   12" × 2"

C   12" × ½"

Assembly Instructions

1. Using one 12" × 12" cardstock as your base, attach piece A to the center of the page.

2. Attach piece B, placing it 2" from the left edge of the page, keeping the top and bottom flush.

3. Attach piece C, placing it directly to the left of piece B, keeping the edges flush.

4. Attach photos, title, and journaling as desired.

Companion Layouts

1b, 1d, 1j, 2g, 3b, 3i, 4e, 5b, 5d, 5h, 6c, 7c, 7g, 8a, 8g

CROSSHATCHING EDGES

A few swipes, and a great new design is born! Using the edge of your stamp pad, swipe the edges of paper in a diagonal motion. Repeat in the opposite direction, creating a crosshatch pattern.

Sidebar–Photo Focus™

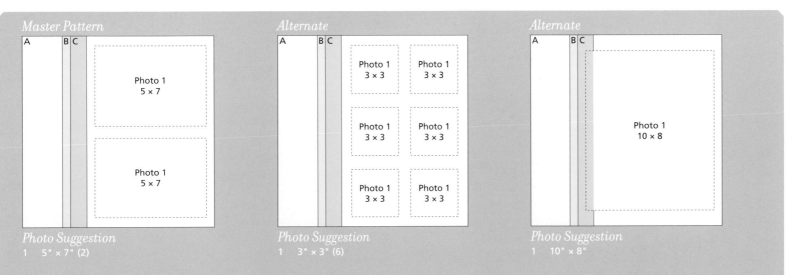

Paper Dimensions

A   12" × 2½"

B   12" × ½"

C   12" × 1"

Assembly Instructions

1. Using one 12" × 12" cardstock as your base, attach piece A to the left side of the page, keeping the edges flush.

2. Attach piece B directly to the right of piece A, keeping the edges flush.

3. Attach piece C directly to the right of piece B, keeping the edges flush.

4. Attach photos, title, and journaling as desired.

Companion Layouts

1b, 1d, 1e, 1i, 2b, 2c, 2e, 2f, 2h, 2k, 6h

STAPLING RIBBON

Lose the glue and try using staples (silver or colored) to fasten ribbon to a layout! These shiny slivers are fast and simple to use, and they'll add both texture and dimension to your pages.

Master Pattern

A | B | C

Photo 1
5 × 7

Photo 1
5 × 7

Photo Suggestion
1   5" × 7" (2)

Alternate

A | B | C

Photo 1
3 × 3

Photo 1
3 × 3

Photo 1
3 × 3

Photo 1
3 × 3

Photo 1
3 × 3

Photo 1
3 × 3

Photo Suggestion
1   3" × 3" (6)

Alternate

A | B | C

Photo 1
10 × 8

Photo Suggestion
1   10" × 8"

3i • Sidebar–Balancing Act™

Paper Dimensions

A 3½" × 7"

B 7" × 7"

C 11" × 3½"

Assembly Instructions

1. Using one 12" × 12" cardstock as your base, attach piece A, placing it ½" from the top and left edges of the page.

2. Attach piece B, placing it ½" from the bottom and left edges of the page.

3. Attach piece C, placing it ½" from the top, bottom, and right edges of the page.

4. Attach photos, title, and journaling as desired.

Companion Layouts

1b, 1c, 2b, 2d, 2f, 2g, 2h, 2i, 2l, 3b, 3d, 3f, 4a, 4e, 4h, 4k, 4l, 4m, 5a, 5d, 6b, 7c, 7g, 7j, 8a, 8e, 8g, 9a, 10a, 10c

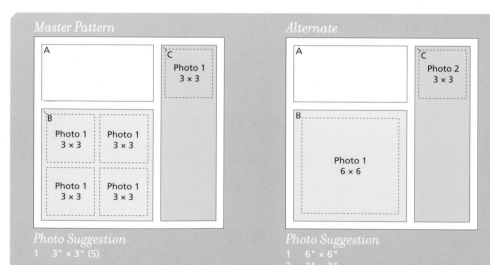

Master Pattern

| A | | C |
| Photo 1 3 × 3 |

| B | Photo 1 3 × 3 | Photo 1 3 × 3 |
| Photo 1 3 × 3 | Photo 1 3 × 3 |

Photo Suggestion
1 3" × 3" (5)

Alternate

| A | | C |
| Photo 2 3 × 3 |

| B | Photo 1 6 × 6 |

Photo Suggestion
1 6" × 6"
2 3" × 3"

BLURRING EFFECT

Sometimes blurred is better! Stamp a sentiment on your layout, then trace over it with a matching colored pencil. Go over it again with a blending pen to produce a lovely blurred effect.

Sidebar–Understated™

Paper Dimensions

A 7½" × 11"

B 3½" × 11"

C 3" × 10½"

D 12" × 1¾"

Assembly Instructions

1. Using one 12" × 12" cardstock as your base, attach piece A, placing it ½" from the top and left edges of the page.

2. Attach piece B directly below piece A, keeping the edges flush.

3. Attach piece C to the center of piece B.

4. Attach piece D 1" from the left edge of the page, keeping the top and bottom flush.

5. Attach photos, title, and journaling as desired.

Companion Layouts

1a, 1c, 1d, 1i, 1j, 2g, 2i, 3b, 3f, 4a, 4l, 4m, 5a, 6a, 6b, 6c, 6h, 6i, 7c, 7g, 7h, 7j, 8d, 8f, 9a, 10a, 10b, 10c, 10d, 10g, 10h

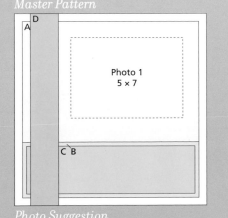

Master Pattern

Photo 1
5 × 7

C B

A D

Photo Suggestion

1   5" × 7"

PHOTO POP

To really make a picture pop, cut a sheet of white cardstock ⅛" larger than the photo size. Center the photo on the piece of paper. With closed scissors, rub the edges of the cardstock, pressing hard until the paper begins to shave off.

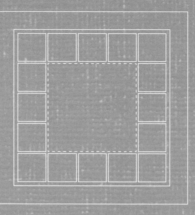

Main Frame™

When I was a little girl, I loved beauty—thanks to my elegant, graceful mother. I was her first child and she took delight styling me in dresses with matching coats and shiny patent leather shoes, ensuring my curls were just right. Even when our family grew, she made each sibling feel as I had felt: like her one and only.

When you have a "one and only" photo, it deserves the rich simplicity of a Main Frame pattern. These patterns highlight one special photo that will reawaken the love of beauty in you—each pattern as pure and uncluttered as your perfect memory.

Jeanette
4 years old

dream

4a • Main Frame—Four Square™

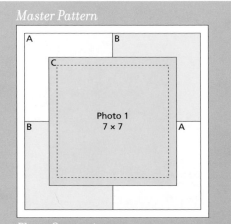

Paper Dimensions

A   5½" × 5½" (2)

B   5½" × 5½" (2)

C   8" × 8"

Master Pattern

A   B
C
Photo 1
7 × 7
B   A

Photo Suggestion

1   7" × 7"

Assembly Instructions

1. Using one 12" × 12" cardstock as your base, attach one piece A, placing it ½" from the top and left edges of the page. Attach remaining piece A, placing it ½" from the bottom and right edges of the page.

2. Attach one piece B directly to the right of upper piece A, placing it ½" from the top and right edges of the page. Attach remaining piece B directly below upper piece A, placing it ½" from the bottom and left edges of the page.

3. Attach piece C to the center of the page.

4. Attach photos, title, and journaling as desired.

Companion Layouts

1a, 1c, 1d, 1e, 1f, 1h, 1i, 1j, 2g, 2i, 2j, 3b, 3f, 3i, 5a, 5b, 5h, 6c, 6f, 7c, 7g, 7j, 8a, 8c, 8e, 8f, 8g, 8j, 9a, 10a, 10g

SCULPTING LETTERS WITH CRAFTING CLAY

This technique will add instant dimension to your artwork! Create any desired shape out of crafting clay; then, using ink of your choice, stamp letters directly onto the clay and allow it to dry. Shade edges using a small sponge, and then attach to your layout.

Main Frame—Quarter Circle™

Paper Dimensions

A   11" × 11"

B   9" × 4"

C   7½" × 5½"

D   5" × 5"

Assembly Instructions

1. Using one 12" × 12" cardstock as your base, attach piece A to the center of the page.

2. Attach piece B, placing it ½" from the top of piece A, keeping the left edges flush.

3. Attach piece C, placing it ½" from the top and left edges of piece B.

4. Cut piece D into a quarter of a circle and attach to the bottom right corner of the page, keeping the edges flush.

5. Attach photos, title, and journaling as desired.

Master Pattern

Photo 1
7 × 5

A
B
C
D

Photo Suggestion

1   7" × 5"

RIBBON WEAVING

Use ribbon to create accents and stitching on baseballs, shoes, or anything that comes stitched. This adds depth, dimension, and tons of fun!

Companion Layouts

1h, 1j, 2f, 2g, 2j, 3b, 3f, 5a, 5c, 5h, 6c, 7g, 7h, 8a, 8c, 8g, 10d

4c • Main Frame–Vertical Window™

Paper Dimensions

A   4" × 12"

B   ½" × 12"

C   8½" × 6½"

Assembly Instructions

1. Using one 12" × 12" cardstock as your base, attach piece A to the top of the page, keeping the side edges flush.

2. Attach piece B directly below piece A, keeping the side edges flush.

3. Attach piece C, placing it 2¼" from the top and 1¼" from the right edge of the page.

4. Attach photos, title, and journaling as desired.

Companion Layouts

1a, 1d, 1h, 2a, 2f, 2g, 2h, 2i, 2j, 2k, 2l, 3a, 3b, 3f, 3h, 3i, 5c, 5d, 5e, 6a, 6b, 6c, 6e, 6f, 6h, 6i, 7a, 7b, 7f, 7j, 8b, 8d, 8f, 8g, 8h, 8j, 9a, 9b, 9c, 10a

CREATIVE TITLES

Be creative with the titles on your page when space is limited. Titles can run vertically, horizontally, or words can even be broken apart to get your message across.

Master Pattern

Photo 1
8 × 6

Photo Suggestion
1   8" × 6"

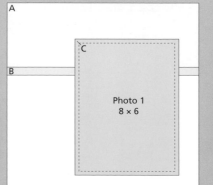

Main Frame—Tied Together™

TRIMMING CHIPBOARD

Cut chipboard alphabets to take on a new and exciting look!

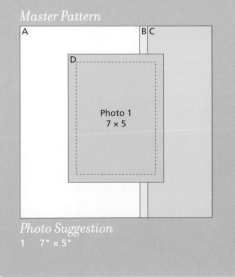

Master Pattern

Photo Suggestion

1   7" × 5"

Paper Dimensions

A   12" × 7½"

B   12" × ½"

C   12" × 4"

D   8" × 6"

Companion Layouts

1a, 1c, 1d, 1f, 1h, 2f, 2g, 2h, 2j, 3b, 3f, 5a, 5c, 5i, 5k, 5l, 6a, 6b, 6f, 6g, 6h, 7a, 7d, 7f, 7j, 8a, 8b, 8c, 8d, 8f, 8h, 8j, 9a, 10d, 10e

Assembly Instructions

1. Using one 12" × 12" cardstock as your base, attach piece A to the left side of the page, keeping the edges flush.

2. Attach piece B directly to the right of piece A, keeping the edges flush.

3. Attach piece C to the right side of the page, keeping the edges flush.

4. Attach piece D, placing it 1¾" from the top and 3" from the side edges of the page.

5. Attach photos, title, and journaling as desired.

4e · Main Frame–Charmed™

Paper Dimensions

A   11" × 8½"

B   7" × 9"

C   2" × 2" (3)

Companion Layouts

1c, 1d, 1e, 1h, 1i, 1j, 2g, 2j, 3b, 3f, 7f, 7g, 7j, 8b, 8c, 8g, 8j, 9a, 10c

Assembly Instructions

1. Using one 12" × 12" cardstock as your base, attach piece A, placing it ½" from the top, bottom, and right edges of the page.

2. Attach piece B, placing it 1" from the top and ½" from the left edge of the page.

3. Attach pieces C, placing them ¾" from the left edge of the page, ½" below piece B, and ¾" from each other.

4. Attach photos, title, and journaling as desired.

ANCHORING HEMP

Add fun texture to your project by placing lengths of hemp in desired positions on your layout, then anchoring them at certain points by hand-stitching them in place.

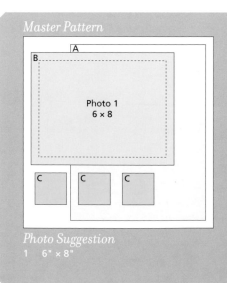

Master Pattern

A

B

Photo 1
6 × 8

C   C   C

Photo Suggestion

1   6" × 8"

Main Frame–Offset™

Paper Dimensions

A   10½" × 10½"

B   10" × 10"

Assembly Instructions

1. Using one 12" × 12" cardstock as your base, attach piece A, placing it ½" from the top and left edges of the page.

2. Attach piece B to the center of piece A.

3. Attach photos, title, and journaling as desired.

Companion Layouts

1a, 1c, 1d, 1e, 1f, 1g, 1h, 1i, 1j, 2a, 2f, 3b, 3d, 3f, 5b, 5c, 5d, 5k, 5l, 6f, 7a, 7f, 7j, 8c, 8f, 8j, 9a, 10a

Master Pattern

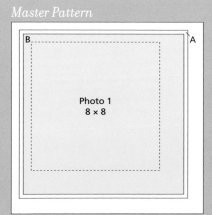

```
B                          A

        Photo 1
         8 × 8
```

Photo Suggestion

1   8" × 8"

RIBBON BORDER

Create an attractive and memorable frame for your layout! Using a piercing tool or a paper punch, make holes around the border of the layout and tie ribbon in knots through the holes to create a ribbon border.

4g · Main Frame—Back Drop™

Paper Dimensions

A   12" × 4"

B   6" × 8"

Assembly Instructions

1. Using one 12" × 12" cardstock as your base, attach piece A, placing it 1" from the left edge of the page, keeping the top and bottom flush.

2. Attach piece B, placing it 1½" from the top and 2" from the left edge of the page.

3. Attach photos, title, and journaling as desired.

Companion Layouts

1a, 1b, 1c, 1d, 1e, 1f, 1g, 1h, 1i, 1j, 2a, 2b, 2c, 2e, 2f, 2g, 2h, 2i, 2j, 2k, 3a, 3b, 3f, 3i, 4a, 4c, 4k, 4m, 5a, 5b, 5c, 5d, 5e, 5f, 5g, 5h, 5k, 5l, 6e, 6f, 6g, 6h, 6i, 7a, 7c, 7e, 7f, 7h, 7j, 8b, 8c, 8d, 8f, 8h, 8j, 9a, 10a, 10b, 10c, 10g, 10h

REVERSE ALPHABET STAMPS

Use an alphabet stamp as a template for page titles. Stamp image on the reverse side of a patterned paper. Cut out the image, then flip it over and attach it to your layout. You've just created instant texture and fun dimension!

Master Pattern

A

B

Photo 1
5 × 7

Photo Suggestion

1   5" × 7"

Main Frame—Tied Up™

Paper Dimensions

A   11" × 11"

B   1½" × 11"

C   8" × 8"

Assembly Instructions

1. Using one 12" × 12" cardstock as your base, attach piece A to the center of the page.

2. Attach piece B, placing it 4½" from the top of piece A, keeping the side edges flush with piece A.

3. Attach piece C to the center of piece A.

4. Attach photos, title, and journaling as desired.

Companion Layouts

1e, 1j, 1h, 2g, 3b, 3f, 3i, 5a, 5g, 5i, 5k, 5l, 6f, 7f, 7i, 7j, 8b, 8c, 8e, 8h, 8j

Master Pattern

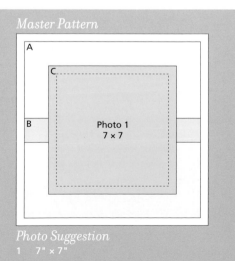

A

C

B

Photo 1
7 × 7

Photo Suggestion

1   7" × 7"

LINEN LAYERING

You can create a delightfully frayed appearance by layering adhesive-backed linen sheets onto cardstock, then scissor distressing the edges. Fraying has never been so fun!

Main Frame–Details™

Paper Dimensions

A 11¾" × 9"

B 3" × 12"

C 8½" × 6½"

Assembly Instructions

1. Using one 12" × 12" cardstock as your base, attach piece A to the bottom of the page, placing it ¼" from the left edge, keeping the bottom flush.

2. Attach piece B, placing it 1½" from the top, keeping the side edges flush.

3. Attach piece C, placing it ¼" from the top and left edges of piece A.

4. Attach photos, title, and journaling as desired.

Companion Layouts

2k, 3d, 6i

Master Pattern

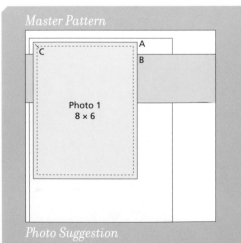

Photo 1
8 × 6

Photo Suggestion

1   8" × 6"

CARDSTOCK PHOTO CORNERS

Cut a square of cardstock and fold it in half, forming a triangle. Stitch it closed to create a photo corner, and you've got an engaging accessory to add to your layout.

Main Frame–Portrait™

CARDSTOCK FRAME

To add inviting dimension and contrast, cut thin strips of complementary cardstock or patterned paper and adhere in corners to create a frame for your page, or unique mats for photos.

Paper Dimensions

A   1½" × 12"

B   8½" × 12"

C   10½" × 8½"

Assembly Instructions

1. Using one 12" × 12" cardstock as your base, attach piece A to the top of the page, keeping the edges flush.

2. Attach piece B to the bottom of the page, keeping the edges flush.

3. Attach piece C to the left side of the page, placing it ¾" from the top, keeping the left edges flush.

4. Attach photos, title, and journaling as desired.

Companion Layouts

1h, 1j

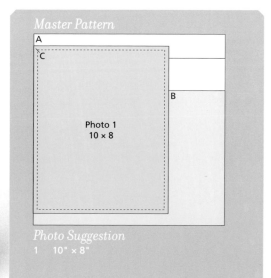

Master Pattern

A

C

B

Photo 1
10 × 8

Photo Suggestion

1   10" × 8"

4k • Main Frame—Quilt Blocks™

Paper Dimensions

A   9¾" × 9¾"

B   1¾" × 1¾" (4)

C   1¾" × 1¾" (4)

D   1¾" × 1¾" (4)

E   1¾" × 1¾" (4)

Assembly Instructions

1. Using one 12" x 12" cardstock as your base, attach piece A to the center of the page.

2. Attach pieces B, C, D, and E in an alternating pattern ¼" from the outside edges of piece A.

3. Attach photos, title, and journaling as desired.

Companion Layouts

1j, 3f, 5l, 6c, 8c

PAPER CRINKLING

Here's an easy way to add dimension to any project. Spray a sheet of cardstock with water. Crinkle paper until the desired texture is achieved, then smooth it out a bit and let it dry. Swipe a round sponge across a stamp pad and then over the paper. With an iron on low heat, press the paper to flatten. Adhere the paper to a sheet of cardstock and cut to desired size.

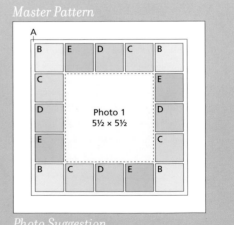

Master Pattern

A

B	E	D	C	B
C				E
D		Photo 1 5½ × 5½		D
E				C
B	C	D	E	B

Photo Suggestion
1   5½" × 5½"

Main Frame—Perfect Square™

Paper Dimensions

A   11" × 11"

B   9" × 9"

Assembly Instructions

1. Using one 12" × 12" cardstock as your base, attach piece A to the center of the page.

2. Attach piece B to the center of piece A.

3. Attach photos, title, and journaling as desired.

Companion Layouts

3f, 5g, 5l, 6c, 6h, 8b, 8c, 8h, 8i, 8j, 10d

Master Pattern

A

B

Photo 1
8 × 8

Photo Suggestion

1   8" × 8"

DISTRESSING WITH RE-INKER

A little brush of ink can make all the difference! Squeeze dark brown re-inker into a craft jar, then dip a stipple brush into the ink. Run the brush along a scrap piece of paper and then quickly brush the layout paper just along the edges, toward the center. Repeat until the desired look is achieved. Let dry.

Main Frame–Border Cutout™

Paper Dimensions

A   11" × 11"

Assembly Instructions

1. Cut an 8" × 8" square from the center of piece A, leaving a 1½" border.

2. Using one 12" × 12" cardstock as your base, attach piece A to the center of the page.

3. Attach photos, title, and journaling as desired.

Companion Layouts

3f, 5g, 5l, 6c, 6h, 8b, 8c, 8h, 8i, 8j, 10d

PAPER FRAME

Here's an exciting way to frame photos or accessories and add unique dimension at the same time! Feed widths of cardstock through a sewing machine, stitching and gathering as you go, then crinkling up for more dimension. Fashion into a frame of desired size.

Master Pattern

A

Photo 1
7 × 7

Photo Suggestion

1   7" × 7"

Main Frame—Wrap Around™

Paper Dimensions

A   3" × 9"

B   9" × 3"

C   3" × 9"

D   9" × 3"

Assembly Instructions

1. Using one 12" × 12" cardstock as your base, attach piece A to the top of the page, keeping the top and left edges flush.

2. Attach piece B to the left side of the page, keeping the bottom and left edges flush.

3. Attach piece C to the bottom of the page, keeping the bottom and right edges flush.

4. Attach piece D to the right side of the page, keeping the top and right edges flush.

5. Attach photos, title, and journaling as desired.

Companion Layouts

1b, 1i, 2k, 3b, 3f, 5a, 5c, 5g, 5k, 6f, 6i, 9a

Master Pattern

A   D

B

Photo
5 × 5

C

Photo Suggestion

1   5" × 5"

TWISTING SPIRAL CLIPS

C'mon baby, let's do the twist! Spiral clips of any size or color can be fashioned into many different shapes and looks. Just use your imagination with these flexible accessories, and you'll come up with ingenious ways to enhance any project!

Front & Center™

How do you portray pure vibrance on a page? That's my challenge every time I scrapbook my daughter Rachel, a young woman who radiates joy, light, and sheer passion for life. She's a magnet for friends and a natural in front of a camera.

The solution is easy: I make her the center of attention, using one of my Front & Center patterns. Front & Center patterns shine the spotlight on your photos, using embellishments to support but never upstage. The result: radiance as real as Rachel herself!

Front & Center—Blocks™

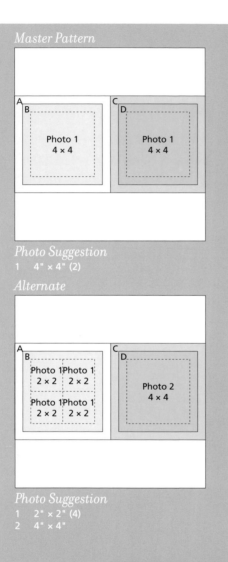

Master Pattern

A
B
Photo 1
4 × 4

C
D
Photo 1
4 × 4

Photo Suggestion

1   4" × 4" (2)

Alternate

A
B
Photo 1
2 × 2
Photo 1
2 × 2
Photo 1
2 × 2
Photo 1
2 × 2

C
D
Photo 2
4 × 4

Photo Suggestion

1   2" × 2" (4)
2   4" × 4"

THE SAME BUT DIFFERENT

When you use multiple accents—brads, spiral clips, conchos, hinges, etc.—of the same color on a page, the results can be dramatic! While the color infuses your page with a welcome congruence, the varied accents make it come alive with interest and originality. It's a fabulous combination!

Paper Dimensions

A   6" × 6"

B   5" × 5"

C   6" × 6"

D   5" × 5"

Assembly Instructions

1. Using one 12" × 12" cardstock as your base, attach piece A, placing it 3" from the top of the page, keeping the left edges flush.

2. Attach piece B to the center of piece A.

3. Attach piece C, placing it 3" from the top of the page, keeping the right edges flush.

4. Attach piece D to the center of piece C.

5. Attach photos, title, and journaling as desired.

Companion Layouts

1g, 1h, 4j, 4l, 4m, 5a (rotated), 5f, 5h, 6b, 6d, 6f, 6h, 8a, 8c, 8d, 8f

Front & Center—Space™

Paper Dimensions

A 10" × 8"

B 12" × 4"

C 6" × 12"

Assembly Instructions

1. Using one 12" × 12" cardstock as your base, attach piece A, placing it 1½" from the top of the page, keeping the left edges flush.

2. Attach piece B to the right side of the page, keeping the right edges flush.

3. Attach piece C, placing it 2" from the top of the page, keeping the side edges flush.

4. Attach photos, title, and journaling as desired.

Companion Layouts

1e, 2f, 3b, 4d, 4h, 4l, 4m, 5d, 7e, 7j, 8g, 9a

A STITCH IN TITLE

For a stunning effect on any page, try hand stitching your title using hemp, waxed flax, thread, embroidery floss, or another fiber of your choice. Your creation will be one-of-a-kind!

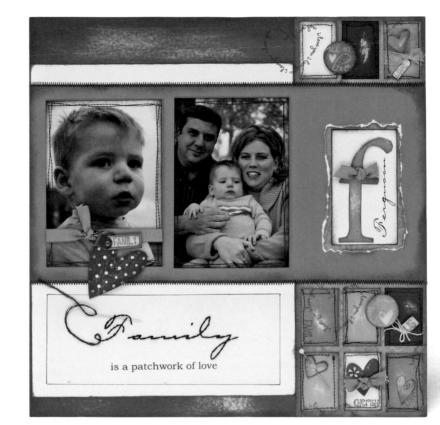

Family is a patchwork of love

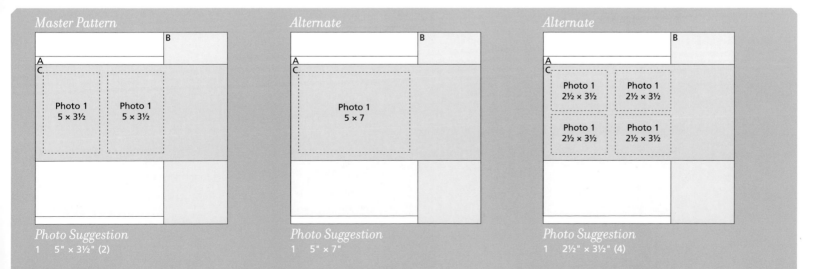

Master Pattern	Alternate	Alternate
Photo 1 5 × 3½ / Photo 1 5 × 3½	Photo 1 5 × 7	Photo 1 2½ × 3½ / Photo 1 2½ × 3½ / Photo 1 2½ × 3½ / Photo 1 2½ × 3½

Photo Suggestion
1   5" × 3½" (2)

Photo Suggestion
1   5" × 7"

Photo Suggestion
1   2½" × 3½" (4)

Front & Center–Trio™

Paper Dimensions

A 12" × 6"

B 5" × 3½" (3)

C 2½" × 5½"

Assembly Instructions

1. Using one 12" × 12" cardstock as your base, attach piece A to the center of the page, placing it 3" from the side edges, keeping the top and bottom flush.

2. Attach pieces B to the page, placing them 1½" from the top, ½" from the side edges, and ¼" from each other.

3. Attach piece C to the page, placing it 1½" from the bottom and centered from side to side. Secure with ribbons if desired.

4. Attach photos, title, and journaling as desired.

Companion Layouts

1d, 1i, 2c, 2e, 2f, 2g, 2h, 2i, 2k, 3a, 3i, 4a, 4c, 4d, 4j, 4k, 4l, 4m, 4n, 6a, 6f, 6g, 6h, 7j, 8f, 8g, 9b

IT'S THE REAL BLING!

It's amazingly simple to make your projects stand out in a crowd. Try brushing chipboard letters and shapes with glue or clear liquid glaze, then sprinkling them with eye-catching glitter.

Master Pattern

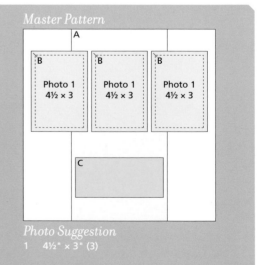

A

B	B	B
Photo 1 4½ × 3	Photo 1 4½ × 3	Photo 1 4½ × 3

C

Photo Suggestion

1 4½" × 3" (3)

Front & Center–Focal™

Paper Dimensions

A   10" × 10½"

B   6" × 4"

Assembly Instructions

1. Using one 12" × 12" cardstock as your base, attach piece A to the page, placing it 1½" from the top, keeping the right edges flush.

2. Attach piece B ½" from the top of piece A, keeping the right edges flush.

3. Attach photos, title, and journaling as desired.

Companion Layouts

1d, 1j, 2j, 3b, 4e, 5b, 8f, 8g

GETTING TO THE CORE

You can create a magical effect on your cardstock pages by "writing" on them with a piercing tool or craft knife. This will scratch away the color, exposing the paper's white core, and you'll have a unique piece of art to call your own!

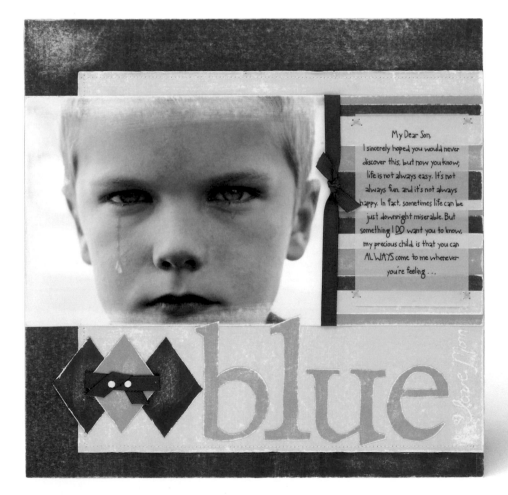

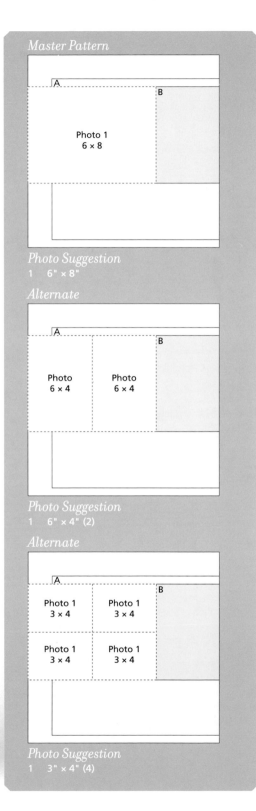

Master Pattern

A

B

Photo 1
6 × 8

Photo Suggestion
1   6" × 8"

Alternate

A

B

Photo
6 × 4

Photo
6 × 4

Photo Suggestion
1   6" × 4" (2)

Alternate

A

B

Photo 1
3 × 4

Photo 1
3 × 4

Photo 1
3 × 4

Photo 1
3 × 4

Photo Suggestion
1   3" × 4" (4)

Front & Center—Split Focus™

Paper Dimensions

A 7" × 12"

B 6" × 12"

C 6" × 2"

D 6" × 3"

E 5" × 5" (2)

F 2½" × 12"

G 1" × 5"

Assembly Instructions

1. Using one 12" × 12" cardstock as your base, attach piece A, placing it 2½" from the top and bottom of the page, keeping the side edges flush.

2. Attach piece B to the center of piece A, keeping the side edges flush.

3. Attach piece C to the left side of piece B, keeping the left edges flush.

4. Attach piece D to piece B, placing it 1½" from the right edge, keeping the top and bottom flush against piece B.

5. Attach one piece E, placing it ½" from the top and left edges of piece B. Attach remaining piece E, placing it ½" from the top and right edges of piece B.

6. Attach piece F to the bottom of the page, keeping the edges flush.

7. Attach piece G to the right edge, placing it ¾" from the bottom, keeping the right edges flush.

8. Attach photos, title, and journaling as desired.

Companion Layouts

4l, 4m, 5e, 5i, 5k, 5l, 6f, 8a, 8c, 8f

RIBBON PHOTO CORNERS

Use any kind of ribbon (the more unique, the better) to create exclusive corners for your photographs. Simply trim a length of ribbon to the correct size and attach it diagonally across each corner of the photo. Your pictures will truly have a corner on originality!

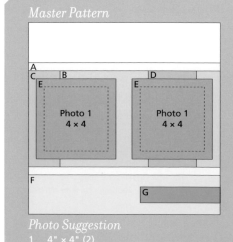

Master Pattern

Photo 1 4 × 4

Photo 1 4 × 4

Photo Suggestion

1 4" × 4" (2)

Front & Center–Mosaic™

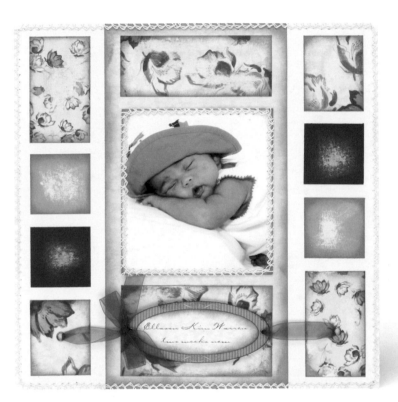

© 2007 JRL Publications

Paper Dimensions

A   12" × 6"

B   2" × 5"

C   3" × 5"

D   3½" × 2" (2)

E   2" × 2" (2)

F   2" × 2" (2)

G   2½" × 2" (2)

Assembly Instructions

1. Using one 12" × 12" cardstock as your base, attach piece A to the center of the page, placing it 3" from the left and right edges, keeping the top and bottom flush.

2. Attach piece B, placing it ½" from the top and side edges of piece A.

3. Attach piece C, placing it ½" from the bottom and side edges of piece A.

4. Attach one set of pieces D, E, F, and G down the left side of the page, placing them ½" from the top, bottom, and left edges of the page, spacing them apart evenly. Attach the remaining set of pieces D, E, F, and G up the right side of the page, placing them ½" from the bottom, top, and right edges, spacing them apart evenly.

5. Attach photos, title, and journaling as desired.

Companion Layouts

1h, 5a, 5f (rotated), 5h, 8c, 8f, 8g, 9a

Master Pattern

D	A B	G
E	Photo 1 5½ × 5	F
F		E
G	C	D

Photo Suggestion

1   5½" × 5"

CROCHET EDGES

If you crochet, you'll love this approach to paper crafting! Using a piercing tool, make evenly spaced holes along one or more edges of your paper and crochet. This simple project dresses a page to perfection!

Front & Center–Accent Band™

CARDSTOCK WEAVE

Your pages might be paper, but it's easy to create lots of texture by weaving strips of paper together like a basket and attaching them to the layout's base cardstock.

Paper Dimensions

A   4½" × 12"

B   3" × 12"

Assembly Instructions

1. Using one 12" × 12" cardstock as your base, attach piece A to the bottom of the page, keeping the edges flush.

2. Attach piece B directly above piece A, keeping the edges flush.

3. Attach photos, title, and journaling as desired.

Companion Layouts

2g, 3b, 4b, 4c, 4d, 4j, 4m, 4n, 5a, 5h, 5i, 6h, 7f

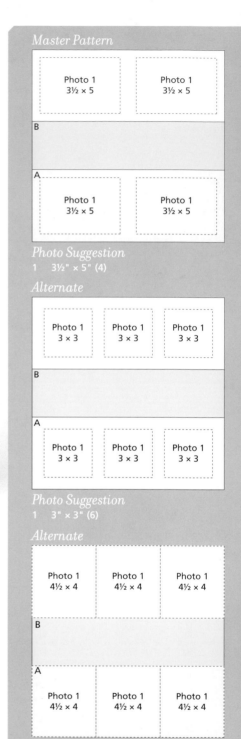

Master Pattern

Photo 1 3½ × 5	Photo 1 3½ × 5

B

A

Photo 1 3½ × 5	Photo 1 3½ × 5

Photo Suggestion

1   3½" × 5" (4)

Alternate

Photo 1 3 × 3	Photo 1 3 × 3	Photo 1 3 × 3

B

A

Photo 1 3 × 3	Photo 1 3 × 3	Photo 1 3 × 3

Photo Suggestion

1   3" × 3" (6)

Alternate

Photo 1 4½ × 4	Photo 1 4½ × 4	Photo 1 4½ × 4

B

A

Photo 1 4½ × 4	Photo 1 4½ × 4	Photo 1 4½ × 4

Photo Suggestion

1   4½" × 4" (6)

Front & Center–Center Stage™

Paper Dimensions

A 11" × 3½"

B 11" × 3½"

C 1½" × 11"

D 11" × 4"

Assembly Instructions

1. Using one 12" × 12" cardstock as your base, attach piece A, placing it ½" from the top, bottom, and left edges of the page.

2. Attach piece B, placing it ½" from the top, bottom, and right edges of the page.

3. Attach piece C, placing it 3½" from the top of the page, keeping the side edges flush with the outside edges of pieces A and B.

4. Attach piece D between pieces A and B, over piece C, keeping the edges flush.

5. Attach photos, title, and journaling as desired.

MINI ACCENTS

If you feel the need to go "miniature" with some of your layout accessories, it's easy to do! For example, cut a length of ribbon in half lengthwise to make smaller-than-normal bows, knots, borders, etc. With a good pair of scissors, size is no object!

Companion Layouts

1a, 1c, 1d, 2c, 2f, 2g, 2i, 2k, 3b, 3f, 3i, 4a, 4c, 4d, 4j, 4l, 4m, 4n, 5a, 5h, 5g, 5i, 5k, 7c, 7f, 7j, 8a, 8d, 8e, 9a, 10a

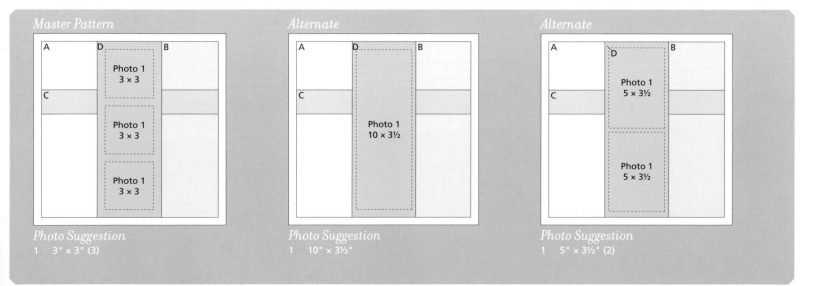

Master Pattern

Photo 1 3 × 3
Photo 1 3 × 3
Photo 1 3 × 3

Photo Suggestion
1   3" × 3" (3)

Alternate

Photo 1 10 × 3½

Photo Suggestion
1   10" × 3½"

Alternate

Photo 1 5 × 3½
Photo 1 5 × 3½

Photo Suggestion
1   5" × 3½" (2)

Front & Center—In the Middle™

Paper Dimensions

A   3" × 12"

B   8" × 2"

C   1" × 12"

Assembly Instructions

1. Using one 12" × 12" cardstock as your base, attach piece A to the top of the page, keeping the edges flush.

2. Attach piece B to the left side of the page directly below piece A, keeping the left edges flush.

3. Attach piece C to the bottom of the page, keeping the edges flush.

4. Attach photos, title, and journaling as desired.

Companion Layouts

1h, 3a, 3b, 3f, 3h, 4d, 4j, 4l, 4m, 5a, 5e, 5i, 5l, 6e, 8a, 8b

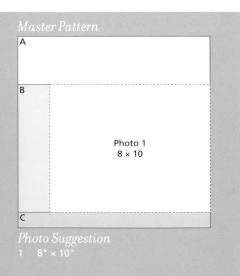

IMAGE POPPING

To make a particular item in your photograph pop, cut it out using scissors or a paper trimmer, then place a narrow mat around it and re-attach it to the photo. This creates a great focal point.

Master Pattern

A

B

Photo 1
8 × 10

C

Photo Suggestion

1   8" × 10"

Front & Center–Main Idea™

CHALK POPPING

Rubbing chalk over a stamped image while it is still slightly damp will make the image stand out beautifully. Experiment with various colors, and choose one that captures your attention.

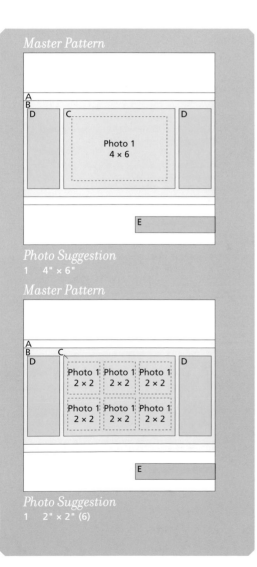

Master Pattern

Photo Suggestion
1   4" × 6"

Master Pattern

Photo Suggestion
1   2" × 2" (6)

Paper Dimensions

A   7" × 12"

B   6" × 12"

C   5" × 7"

D   5" × 2" (2)

E   1" × 5"

Companion Layouts

3b, 3f, 8c

Assembly Instructions

1. Using one 12" × 12" cardstock as your base, attach piece A, placing it 2½" from the top and bottom of the page, keeping the side edges flush.

2. Attach piece B to the center of piece A, keeping the side edges flush.

3. Attach piece C to the center of piece B.

4. Attach one piece D to piece B, to the left of piece C, centering it in the space. Attach remaining piece D to piece B, to the right of piece C, centering it in the space.

5. Attach piece E, placing it ¾" from the bottom, keeping the right edges flush.

6. Attach photos, title, and journaling as desired.

Front & Center–Basic™

Paper Dimensions

A   7" × 12"

B   6" × 12"

Assembly Instructions

1. Using one 12" × 12" cardstock as your base, attach piece A, placing it 2½" from the top and bottom of the page, keeping the side edges flush.

2. Attach piece B to the center of piece A, keeping the side edges flush.

3. Attach photos, title, and journaling as desired.

Companion Layouts

2c, 3a, 3b, 3f, 3h, 4a, 4d, 4j, 4l, 4m, 5a, 5e, 5g, 5h, 5k, 5l, 6b, 6d, 6f, 6h, 7d, 8a, 8c, 8d, 8g, 8j

BULL'S-EYE

There's nothing like a well-placed arrow to accentuate a focal point or draw attention to images in a photo. These can be hand-drawn, ready-made stickers, fashioned from chipboard shapes, or cut from self-adhesive artwork. Whatever your preference, the arrow points to all things important!

Master Pattern

A
B

| Photo 1 5 × 3½ | Photo 1 5 × 3½ | Photo 1 5 × 3½ |

Photo Suggestion
1   5" × 3½" (3)

Alternate

A
B

Photo 1 10 × 8

Photo Suggestion
1   10" × 8"

Alternate

A
B

| Photo 1 4 × 4 | Photo 1 4 × 4 | Photo 1 4 × 4 |

Photo Suggestion
1   4" × 4" (3)

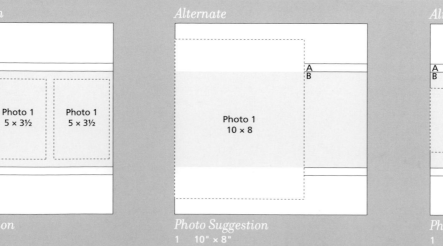
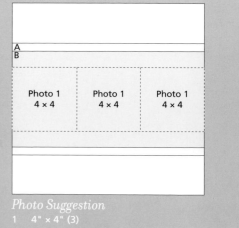

Front & Center–Photo Focus™

Paper Dimensions

A 7" × 12"

B 6" × 12"

C 4" × 5½" (3)

Assembly Instructions

1. Using one 12" × 12" cardstock as your base, attach piece A, placing it 2½" from the top and bottom of the page, keeping the side edges flush.

2. Attach piece B to the center of piece A, keeping the side edges flush.

3. Attach one piece C, placing it 1¾" from the top and 1¼" from the left edge of the page. Attach the second piece C, placing it ¼" below the first. Attach remaining piece C, placing it ¼" from the top of piece B and ½" from the right edge.

4. Attach photos, title, and journaling as desired.

Companion Layouts

2k, 3b, 4d, 4j, 4l, 4m, 4n, 5a, 5e, 5i, 5k, 6d, 6h, 8f, 8g

Master Pattern

A	
B	
C	
Photo 1 3½ × 5	C
C	Photo 2 5 × 3½
Photo 1 3½ × 5	

Photo Suggestion

1 3½" × 5" (2)
2 5" × 3½"

ALL DISTRESSED IN WHITE

A distressed page is not always dark around the edges! For a fun and refreshing distressed look, try swiping the edges of colored cardstock with white ink or paint. It's charming!

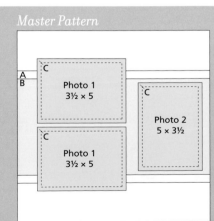

Half & Half™

I am blessed to be many women: mother, wife, friend, sister, neighbor, entrepreneur, innovator, artist, and now, nana. I found immediate joy in every role, but finding balance among them has been a lifelong pursuit. There is art in a balanced life, and it has required a fierce commitment to priorities and a willingness to draw boundaries.

Similarly, a layout's appeal lies in its ability to maintain visual balance—each element kept in priority and proportion. Achieving balance in your art needn't be a lifelong pursuit. The Half & Half patterns perfectly balance everything you want in your life and your layouts—people, art, stories, and personality—without ever compromising composition.

Half & Half—Corner Title™

Paper Dimensions

A   12" × 6"

B   2" × 6"

C   7" × 5"

D   12" × 5"

Assembly Instructions

1. Using one 12" × 12" cardstock as your base, attach piece A to the left side of the page, keeping the edges flush.

2. Attach piece B, placing it 1" from the top, keeping the side edges flush with piece A.

3. Attach piece C, placing it ½" from the bottom and ½" from the left edge of the page.

4. Attach piece D, placing it ½" from the right edge of the page, keeping the top and bottom flush.

5. Attach photos, title, and journaling as desired.

Companion Layouts

1e, 1h, 1i, 2c, 2g, 3a, 3f, 5a, 5g, 5i, 5k, 7d

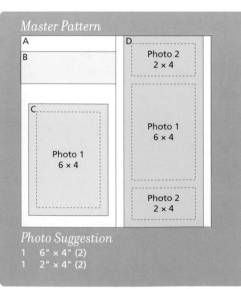

Master Pattern

A

B

D

Photo 2
2 × 4

C

Photo 1
6 × 4

Photo 1
6 × 4

Photo 2
2 × 4

Photo Suggestion

1   6" × 4" (2)

1   2" × 4" (2)

STITCHING WITH NATURAL HEMP

Many thick fibers are created using multiple strands of that fiber wrapped around itself. To separate a single strand, twist a length of hemp, embroidery floss, etc. in the opposite direction from its weave. Use the single strand and stitch where desired. You'll have a one-of-a-kind design!

Half & Half—Split Focus™

Paper Dimensions

A   12" × 6"

B   11" × 5"

C   1" × 6"

D   1¼" × 1¼"

Assembly Instructions

1. Using one 12" × 12" cardstock as your base, attach piece A to the right side of the page, keeping the edges flush.

2. Attach piece B to the center of piece A.

3. Attach piece C to the left side of the page, placing it 5½" from the top, keeping the left edges flush.

4. Attach piece D to the center of piece C.

5. Attach photos and journaling as desired.

Companion Layouts

1h, 2b, 2k, 3d, 3e, 4m, 5a, 6b (rotated), 6d, 6f, 7b, 7c, 8c, 8d, 8f

Master Pattern

Photo 1 5 × 2½	Photo 1 5 × 2½

C   D

Photo 1 5 × 2½	Photo 1 5 × 2½

A
B
Photo 2 4 × 4

Photo Suggestion
1   5" × 2½" (4)
2   4" × 4"

Alternate

Photo 1 4½ × 5

C   D

Photo 1 4½ × 5

A
B

Photo 2 3 × 4

Photo 2 3 × 4

Photo 2 3 × 4

Photo Suggestion
1   4½" × 5" (2)
2   3" × 4" (3)

ACCENTING JOURNAL STRIPS

Using hemp knots to accent your journal strips will add interest to your artwork and your story! You can tie the knots around the edges of the strips, place one or more in any blank spaces, or cluster them at one or both ends to add dimension.

Half & Half—Top Focus™

Paper Dimensions

A 11" × 5"

B 11" × 5"

Assembly Instructions

1. Using one 12" × 12" cardstock as your base, attach piece A, placing it ½" from the top and ¾" from the left edge of the page.

2. Attach piece B, placing it ½" from the top and ¾" from the right edge of the page.

3. Attach photos, title, and journaling as desired.

Companion Layouts

1c, 1d, 2k, 4h, 4k, 4l, 4m, 4n, 5a, 5k, 6c (rotated), 6d, 6f, 7c, 7e, 7g, 8c, 8f, 9a, 9c, 10a, 10e, 10h

RANDOM SEWING

Create a unique background paper by random machine stitching on cardstock. Create swirls, loops, straight lines, and more . . . use your imagination and see where the stitching takes you!

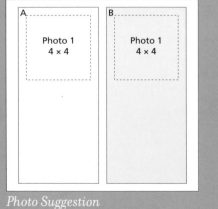

Master Pattern

A	B
Photo 1 4 × 4	Photo 1 4 × 4

Photo Suggestion

1   4" × 4" (2)

Half & Half–Perfect Square™

Paper Dimensions

A   12" × 6"

B   12" × ½"

C   9" × 9"

D   1½" × 1½" (2 cut diagonally)

Assembly Instructions

1. Using one 12" × 12" cardstock as your base, attach piece A to the right side of the page, keeping the edges flush.

2. Attach piece B, centering it over the left edge of piece A, keeping the top and bottom flush.

3. Attach piece C to the center of the page.

4. Attach photos, title, and journaling as desired.

5. Attach pieces D to the photo as photo corners.

Companion Layouts

1d, 1e, 1h, 1j, 2k, 3e, 3f, 5a, 5c, 5h, 5k, 6b, 6d (rotated), 6f, 7c, 7d, 7f, 8a, 8b, 8c, 8d, 8e, 8f, 8g, 8j, 9a, 9b, 9c, 10a, 10b

COVERING CHIPBOARD WITH ADHESIVE-BACKED SHEETS

Add fantastic texture and dimension to any chipboard shape by covering it with vellum, twill, or linen adhesive-backed sheets. To create even greater interest and make the shapes pop, random stamp the sheets with images and colors of your choice before covering the chipboard.

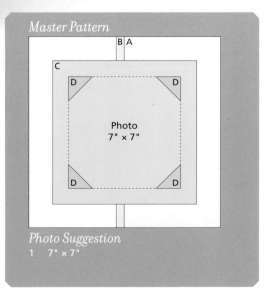

Master Pattern

B A

C

D   D

Photo
7" × 7"

D   D

Photo Suggestion
1   7" × 7"

Half & Half–Tags™

DYEING PAPER FLOWERS

You can dye paper flowers to match any color in your layout. Just add water and re-inker to a craft jar, dip the flowers, and let them dry. It's bloomin' simple!

Paper Dimensions

A   12" × 6"

B   12" × 3½"

C   3" × 5¾" (3)

Companion Layouts

1a, 1b, 3b, 4d, 4h, 4m, 5c, 5g, 5h, 5i, 5k, 6b, 6e (rotated), 6h, 7f, 7i, 7j, 8d, 8h, 9a, 9b, 9c, 9d

Assembly Instructions

1. Using one 12" × 12" cardstock as your base, attach piece A to the right side of the page, keeping the edges flush.

2. Attach piece B to the center of piece A.

3. Attach pieces C, placing them ¾" from the top and bottom of the page and ¾" from each other, keeping the left edges flush.

4. Attach photos, title, and journaling as desired.

Master Pattern

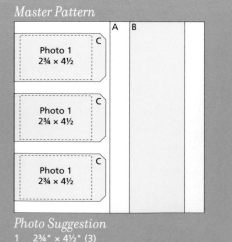

		A	B
Photo 1 2¾ × 4½	C		
Photo 1 2¾ × 4½	C		
Photo 1 2¾ × 4½	C		

Photo Suggestion

1   2¾" × 4½" (3)

is the girl who lives next door. She's lived there all of Kenyon's life. She plays street hockey, jumps the bike ramp, even collects spiders and rocks. Kenyon sees her as "one of the guys".

I hope it's not terribly soon that Kenyon notices, as I have, how beautiful Ally is becoming. Perhaps it's already happened. I noticed this when I asked them to pose for a picture. I felt their sudden shyness to be next to each other. How adorable! I'll have to keep my eye on these two over the coming years.

What a beautiful thing for my son to have such a wonderful relationship with "The Girl Next Door"

Half & Half—4 Photo™

Paper Dimensions

A 12" × 6"

B 5" × 5" (4)

Assembly Instructions

1. Using one 12" × 12" cardstock as your base, attach piece A to the left side of the page, keeping the edges flush.

2. Attach pieces B, placing them ½" from the top and side edges of the page.

3. Attach photos, title, and journaling as desired.

Companion Layouts

2e, 2l, 3d, 3f, 4a, 4h, 4l, 4m, 4n, 5a, 5h, 6b, 6d, 9a

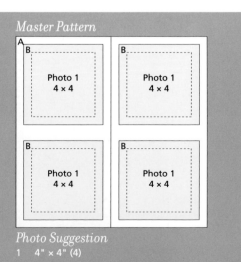

GLAZE-FILLED CONCHOS

Once you've attached a concho to your layout, you can add extra "bling" by filling it with clear liquid glaze and adding glitter as desired. It's a great way to make the page pop!

Master Pattern

A
B
Photo 1
4 × 4

B
Photo 1
4 × 4

B
Photo 1
4 × 4

B
Photo 1
4 × 4

Photo Suggestion

1   4" × 4" (4)

6g · *Half & Half–Combination*™

It's not easy for a first time MOM to put her first born SON on a bus on his first day of kindergarten and then just watch him drive away, COMPLETELY on his own... (for the first time)

Kindergarten

Waiting...

...but aren't you proud of me? I did it. I stood there and watched you drive away, (and then I jumped in the car and followed you all the way to school!)

Paper Dimensions

A 12" × 6"

B 1½" × 12"

C 4" × 4" (2)

D 4" Circle

Assembly Instructions

1. Using one 12" × 12" cardstock as your base, attach piece A to the left side of the page, keeping the edges flush.

2. Attach piece B, placing it 2" from the top of the page, keeping the side edges flush.

3. Attach one piece C, placing it 1½" from the bottom and 1" from the left edge of the page.

4. Attach the remaining piece C, placing it 4" from the top and 1" from the right edge of the page.

5. Attach piece D, placing it 1" from the top and centered on the page from side to side.

6. Attach photos, title, and journaling as desired.

Companion Layouts

2k, 2l, 3b, 4c

MINI ALBUM

Using file folder templates and cardstock, you can create an adorable mini book to add more pictures or journaling to a layout. Include more in less space!

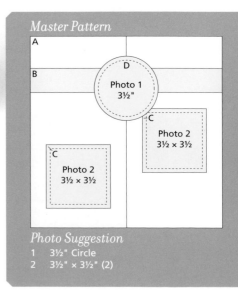

Master Pattern

A

B

D

Photo 1
3½"

C

Photo 2
3½ × 3½

C

Photo 2
3½ × 3½

Photo Suggestion

1 3½" Circle

2 3½" × 3½" (2)

Half & Half–Balanced™

Paper Dimensions

A   12" × 6"

B   8" × 6"

C   ½" × 6"

Assembly Instructions

1. Using one 12" × 12" cardstock as your base, attach piece A to the left side of the page, keeping the edges flush.

2. Attach piece B to the bottom right corner of the page, keeping the edges flush.

3. Attach piece C, placing it 3" from the top, keeping the right edges flush.

4. Attach photos, title, and journaling as desired.

Companion Layouts

1a, 1e, 2e, 2h, 2j, 3b, 3h, 3j, 4d, 5g, 5k, 6h (rotated), 7f, 9a, 9d

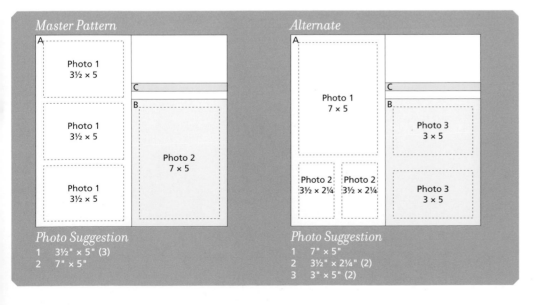

Master Pattern

A

Photo 1
3½ × 5

C

B

Photo 1
3½ × 5

Photo 2
7 × 5

Photo 1
3½ × 5

Photo Suggestion
1   3½" × 5" (3)
2   7" × 5"

Alternate

A

Photo 1
7 × 5

C

B

Photo 3
3 × 5

Photo 2
3½ × 2¼

Photo 2
3½ × 2¼

Photo 3
3 × 5

Photo Suggestion
1   7" × 5"
2   3½" × 2¼" (2)
3   3" × 5" (2)

CREATING FRAMES WITH HEMP

Natural hemp is a perfect fiber for adding texture and dimension to a layout. To create delightful frames for photos, journaling, or titles, using craft glue, simply adhere one or more lengths of hemp around their edges.

Half & Half—Simple Frames™

Paper Dimensions

A   12" × 6"

B   7" × 5"

C   7" × 5"

D   2½" × 5" (2)

Assembly Instructions

1. Using one 12" × 12" cardstock as your base, attach piece A to the right side of the page, keeping the edges flush.

2. Attach piece B, placing it ½" from the top and right edges of the page.

3. Attach piece C, placing it ½" from the top and left edges of the page.

4. Attach one piece D, placing it 1" from the bottom and ½" from the left edge of the page.

5. Attach remaining piece D, placing it 1" from the bottom and ½" from the right edge of the page.

6. Attach photos, title, and journaling as desired.

Companion Layouts

1d, 1i, 2e, 3f, 4j, 5i, 6i (rotated), 7d, 8b, 8h, 9a

Master Pattern

C	A B
Photo 1 6 × 4	Photo 1 6 × 4
D	D

Photo Suggestion

1   6" × 4" (2)

CREATING DIMENSIONAL LETTERS USING LARGE ALPHABET STAMPS

Create stand-out letters in a flash! Stamp large alphabet letters on cardstock. Cut out each letter and set aside. Adhere two sheets of white cardstock together. Spread glue over the stamped letters and adhere to the double sheet of paper. Cut letters out again using a craft knife. Scissor distress the edges of the letters.

Half & Half—It's Sixes™

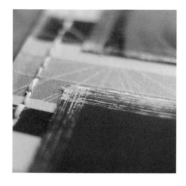

Paper Dimensions

A 11" × 5½"

B 11" × 5½"

C 11" × 4½"

Companion Layouts

1i, 3j, 4e, 4l, 4m

Assembly Instructions

1. Using one 12" × 12" cardstock as your base, attach piece A, placing it ½" from the top, bottom, and left edges of the page.

2. Attach piece B, placing it ½" from the top, bottom, and right edges of the page.

3. Attach piece C to piece B, placing it ½" from the left edge, keeping the top and bottom flush.

4. Attach photos, title, and journaling as desired.

PHOTO DISTRESSING

For an enchanting distressed look, quickly swipe along edges of a photo using rough-grit sandpaper. Just this little bit of effort will create a wonderful new ambience for your layout!

Master Pattern

A		B	C
Photo 1 3 × 5			Photo 2 3 × 3
Photo 1 3 × 5			Photo 2 3 × 3
Photo 1 3 × 5			Photo 2 3 × 3

Photo Suggestion

1 3" × 5" (3)

2 3" × 3" (3)

Triple Play™

I often say that my youngest child, Aubrey, saved my life. She was born at a time when my scrapbooking company was booming, and I was spending long hours at work. She didn't care a lick about mommy's job, just mommy. She'd extend her arms and stare up at me with big, blue eyes, just begging to be held. I'd pick her up, and put the world aside.

This layout using a Triple Play pattern reminds me of that little girl who was my lifeline—my connection to what's important and lasting. Scrapbooking can be that tether for us all, as we use our hands to connect to what's in our hearts.

Triple Play–Triple Tagline™

Master Pattern

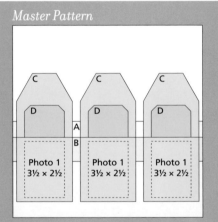

Photo Suggestion

1   3½" × 2½" (3)

LAYERING PAPER FLOWERS

To make paper flowers really blossom on a
layout, layer them by starting with a larger
flower on the bottom and attaching progres-
sively smaller flowers on top of each other.
This will give your page a uniquely dimensional look.

Paper Dimensions

A   6" × 12"

B   1½" × 12"

C   12" × 3½" (3)

D   6" × 2½" (3)

Companion Layouts

1i, 2b, 2e, 2l, 3a, 3b, 3f, 4a, 4c, 4d, 4f, 4h, 5d,
5h, 7a, 8g, 9a

Assembly Instructions

1. Using one 12" × 12" cardstock as your base,
    attach piece A to the bottom of the page,
    keeping the edges flush.

2. Attach piece B, placing it 1" from the top of
    piece A, keeping the side edges flush.

3. Leaving an 8" base, fold the bottom of pieces
    C up 4", adhering only the side edges in
    order to form a pocket. Attach pieces C to
    the page, placing them ¼" from the sides, 1"
    from the bottom, and ½" from each other.

4. Insert pieces D into the piece C pockets.

5. Attach photos, title, and journaling as desired.

Triple Play—Tagline™

Paper Dimensions

A   4" × 12"

B   ½" × 12"

C   7½" × 12"

D   8½" × 5"

E   4" × 4" (2)

Assembly Instructions

1. Using one 12" × 12" cardstock as your base, attach piece A to the top of the page, keeping the edges flush.

2. Attach piece B directly below piece A, keeping the edges flush.

3. Attach piece C to the bottom of the page, keeping the edges flush.

4. Attach piece D, placing it 2½" from the top and 1" from the left edge of the page.

5. Attach pieces E, placing them 2½" from the top, 1" from the right edge, and ½" from each other.

6. Attach photos, title, and journaling as desired.

Companion Layouts

1i, 2k, 3a, 3f, 4c, 4d, 4m, 5d, 5h, 5k, 5l, 6i, 7f, 8f, 9a

Master Pattern

A

D

B

C

E
Photo 2
3½ × 3½

Photo 1
5½ × 4

E
Photo 2
3½ × 3½

Photo Suggestion

1   5½" × 4"

2   3½" × 3½" (2)

INKING TEXTURED CARDSTOCK

Just add ink, and the results will be stunning! You can ink textured cardstock with coordinating color to enhance its textured look. Try using a small paint brush, a sponge, a stipple brush or swiping the paper across a stamp pad to add color and texture.

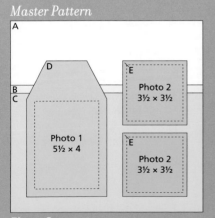

Triple Play

Triple Play—Three Is the Charm™

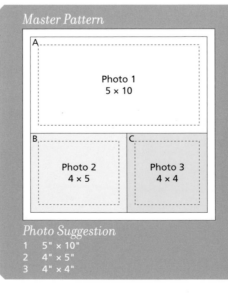

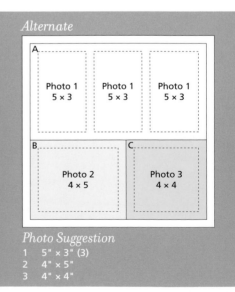

Paper Dimensions

A   6" × 11"

B   5" × 6"

C   5" × 5"

Assembly Instructions

1. Using one 12" × 12" cardstock as your base, attach piece A, placing it ½" from the top and side edges of the page.

2. Attach piece B to the page, placing it ½" from the bottom and left edges.

3. Attach piece C to the page, placing it ½" from the bottom and right edges.

4. Attach photos, title, and journaling as desired.

Companion Layouts

1d, 1h, 3h, 4d, 6c, 7c (rotated)

ADDING DIMENSION

Using clear liquid glaze on chipboard shapes, cardstock, etc., is a fabulous way to add highlights and dimension. (Note: The glaze often takes some time to dry. Dry accents completely before adhering them to your layout.)

Master Pattern

A	
Photo 1 5 × 10	
B	**C**
Photo 2 4 × 5	**Photo 3** 4 × 4

Photo Suggestion

1   5" × 10"
2   4" × 5"
3   4" × 4"

Alternate

A		
Photo 1 5 × 3	**Photo 1** 5 × 3	**Photo 1** 5 × 3
B		**C**
Photo 2 4 × 5		**Photo 3** 4 × 4

Photo Suggestion

1   5" × 3" (3)
2   4" × 5"
3   4" × 4"

Triple Play–Basic™

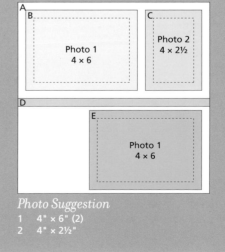

CORNER JACKETS

Here's a way to add an intriguing (and slightly mysterious) dimension to your layout: Cut a square of paper. Fold its corners in and punch holes for eyelets. Tie closed with desired ribbon. Adhere to corner(s) of page.

Master Pattern

A
B — Photo 1 4 × 6
C — Photo 2 4 × 2½
D
E — Photo 1 4 × 6

Photo Suggestion
1   4" × 6" (2)
2   4" × 2½"

Paper Dimensions

A   6" × 12"

B   5" × 7"

C   5" × 3½"

D   ½" × 12"

E   5" × 7"

Companion Layouts

This page is a right-side page only.

Assembly Instructions

1. Using one 12" × 12" cardstock as your base, attach piece A to the top of the page, keeping the edges flush.

2. Attach piece B, placing it ½" from the top and left edges of the page.

3. Attach piece C, placing it ½" from the top and right edges of the page.

4. Attach piece D directly below piece A, keeping the edges flush.

5. Attach piece E, placing it ¼" from the bottom and ½" from the right edge of the page.

6. Attach photos, title, and journaling as desired.

Triple Play–Offset™

Paper Dimensions

A 6" × 12"

B 2" × 12"

C 5" × 5"

D 7" × 5"

Assembly Instructions

1. Using one 12" × 12" cardstock as your base, attach piece A, placing it 1¼" from the top of the page, keeping the side edges flush.

2. Attach piece B, placing it ¾" from the top of piece A, keeping the side edges flush.

3. Attach piece C, placing it ½" from the top of piece A and ¾" from the right edge of the page.

4. Attach piece D, placing it ½" below piece B and ¾" from the left edge of the page.

5. Attach photos, title, and journaling as desired.

Companion Layouts

1a, 1i, 2b, 2c, 2e, 2f, 3a, 3b, 3f, 4d, 4h, 4k, 4l, 4m, 6d, 6i, 7e (rotated), 7f, 7j, 8a, 8f, 8h, 9a, 9b, 9c

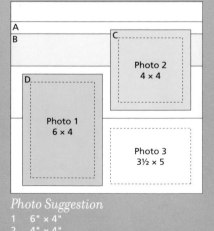

FAUX NAILS

Heads up! Pewter brads can be made to look like nail heads by pounding them with a hammer. Try it—you'll love it!

Master Pattern

A

B

C

Photo 2
4 × 4

D

Photo 1
6 × 4

Photo 3
3½ × 5

Photo Suggestion

1 6" × 4"

2 4" × 4"

3 3½" × 5"

Triple Play—Three of a Kind™

CREATING CUSTOMIZED PATTERNED PAPERS

Putting together your own patterned papers will complement your layout and add a special touch to each page. Just add hole punches, paper flowers, or stripes to your cardstock for a one-of-a-kind background!

Paper Dimensions

A	12" × 4"
B	12" × 4"
C	12" × 4"
D	5½" × 3½" (3)

Assembly Instructions

1. Using one 12" × 12" cardstock as your base, attach piece A to the left side of the page, keeping the edges flush.

2. Attach piece B, placing it directly to the right of piece A, keeping the edges flush.

3. Attach piece C to the right side of the page, keeping the edges flush.

4. Attach pieces D, placing them 1¼" from the top, centered on each piece A, B, and C from side to side.

5. Attach photos, title, and journaling as desired.

Companion Layouts

1c, 1e, 1f, 1i, 2c, 2e, 2f, 2h, 2k, 3b, 3f, 4b, 4f, 4h, 4j, 4l, 6a, 6b, 6h, 7f (rotated), 8g, 9a, 9c

Makayla

Hope

Melody

Cousins 2007

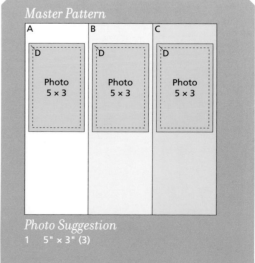

Master Pattern

A	B	C
D	D	D
Photo 5 × 3	Photo 5 × 3	Photo 5 × 3

Photo Suggestion

1   5" × 3" (3)

Triple Play–Columns™

Paper Dimensions

A   11" × 3½"

B   11" × 3½"

C   11" × 3½"

Assembly Instructions

1. Using one 12" × 12" cardstock as your base, attach piece A, placing it ½" from the top and left edges of the page.

2. Attach piece B, placing it ½" from the top and ¼" from piece A.

3. Attach piece C, placing it ½" from the top and right edges of the page.

4. Attach photos, title, and journaling as desired.

Companion Layouts

1d, 1i, 1j, 2c, 2f, 2g, 2h, 3b, 3f, 3i, 4f, 4h, 4l, 4n, 5b, 5h, 6d, 7g (rotated), 8a, 9a, 10c

SHADOWING TITLES

With this useful technique, a little off-center is right on! Stamp a desired title on base cardstock. Stamp the title again on a separate piece of cardstock; cut out. Adhere the cut-out title slightly off center over the top of the first stamped image.

Master Pattern

A	B	C
Photo 1 3 × 3	Photo 1 3 × 3	Photo 1 3 × 3

Photo Suggestion
1   3" × 3" (3)

Alternate

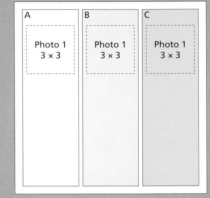
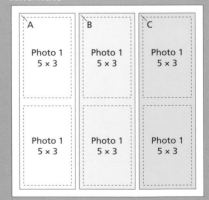

A	B	C
Photo 1 5 × 3	Photo 1 5 × 3	Photo 1 5 × 3
Photo 1 5 × 3	Photo 1 5 × 3	Photo 1 5 × 3

Photo Suggestion
1   5" × 3" (6)

Triple Play—Combination™

Paper Dimensions

A   11" × 11"

B   3½" circle

C   4" × 4" (2)

Assembly Instructions

1.   Using one 12" × 12" cardstock as your base, attach piece A to the center of the page.

2.   Attach piece B and the two pieces C on the page as desired, along with any accent pieces you have chosen.

3.   Attach photos, title, and journaling as desired.

Companion Layouts

This page is a right-side page only.

Master Pattern

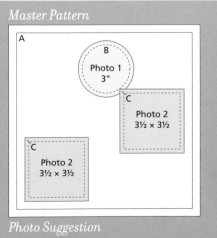

A

B
Photo 1
3"

C
Photo 2
3½ × 3½

C
Photo 2
3½ × 3½

Photo Suggestion

1   3" circle

2   3½" × 3½" (2)

CREATING DECORATIVE BORDERS

Hemp and waxed flax are great for framing photos, journaling, and accessories on your layouts. But don't forget to use them to create decorative borders around the pages themselves. This can add a sophisticated, sporty, and even adventurous feel to your artwork.

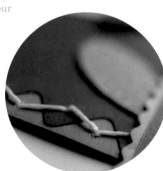

Paper Dimensions

A   5" × 3" (2)

B   6" × 4"

C   4" × 11"

Master Pattern

A — Photo 1 4½ × 2½

B — Photo 2 5 × 3

A — Photo 1 4½ × 2½

C

Photo Suggestion

1   4½" × 2½" (2)

2   5" × 3"

SANDING FOR EFFECT

To create patterned papers with an exotic feel, try using chipboard flowers or other shapes to add subtle images. Simply position a chipboard shape beneath a piece of white core cardstock, then sand the cardstock as desired until the white core appears in the image of the shape. Repeat as many times as you wish to create an intriguing design on the paper.

Assembly Instructions

1. Using one 12" × 12" cardstock as your base, attach one piece A, placing it 1" from the top and ½" from the left side of the page. Attach remaining piece A, placing it 1" from the top and ½" from the right side of the page.

2. Attach piece B, placing it ½" from the top of the page, centered between the pieces A.

3. Attach piece C, placing it ½" from the left, bottom, and right edges of the page.

4. Attach photos, title, and journaling as desired.

Companion Layouts

This page is a right-side page only.

Triple Play—Over the Top™

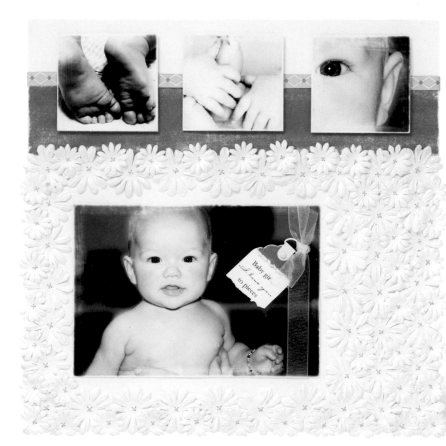

Paper Dimensions

A 3½" × 12"

B 3½" × 3½" (3)

Assembly Instructions

1. Using one 12" × 12" cardstock as your base, attach piece A, placing it 2" from the top of the page, keeping the side edges flush.

2. Attach the three pieces B across piece A, placing them 1" from the top of the page and spacing them evenly from side to side.

3. Attach photos, title, and journaling as desired.

Companion Layouts

1a, 1d, 1i, 2b, 2c, 2e, 2f, 2g, 2h, 2i, 3a, 3b, 3f, 7j (rotated), 8e, 8g, 9a, 10a

Master Pattern

| B Photo 1 3 × 3 | B Photo 1 3 × 3 | B Photo 1 3 × 3 |

A

Photo Suggestion

1   3" × 3" (3)

FLOWER POWER

When you want to add the pizzazz of paper flowers to your layout, it's simple to get them to stay where you put them. Use temporary adhesive to attach the flowers to your cardstock or patterned paper; then a stitch or two in the center of each flower will secure it in place.

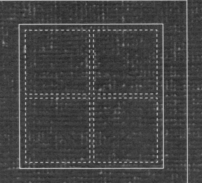

Quartet™

See Belle's sparkling eyes? They are my own. Sense Noah's feisty independence? That's familiar, too. Belle and Noah aren't just my grandchildren, they are my legacy. I watch them at play and their laughter is delicious music—fresh and yet as vintage as my own childhood.

Nothing captures the music of your life like a scrapbook page: this Quartet pattern plays four sweet notes, in harmony with today, even more treasured tomorrow. They say nobody lives forever. But I am a scrapbooker and a nana— I know better.

It's such a *grand* thing to be a mother of a mother - that's why the world calls it grandmother

GRAND KIDS

Quartet–Border Cutout™

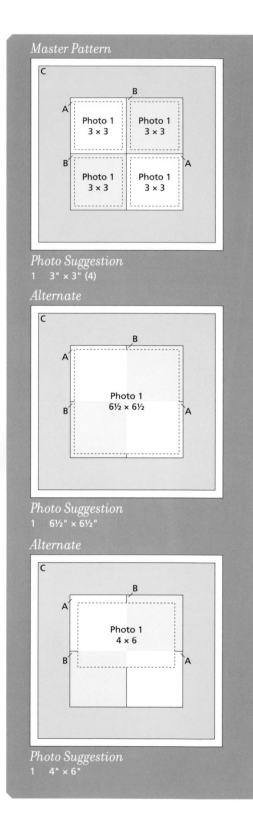

Master Pattern

C

A | B
Photo 1 3 × 3 | Photo 1 3 × 3

B | A
Photo 1 3 × 3 | Photo 1 3 × 3

Photo Suggestion
1   3" × 3" (4)

Alternate

C

A   B
Photo 1 6½ × 6½

B   A

Photo Suggestion
1   6½" × 6½"

Alternate

C

A   B
Photo 1 4 × 6

B   A

Photo Suggestion
1   4" × 6"

Paper Dimensions

A   3½" × 3½" (2)

B   3½" × 3½" (2)

C   11" × 11"

Companion Layouts

This page is a right-side page only.

QUARTERED PHOTOS

To create the visual sensation of observing a scene through a window, cut one main photo into quarters and affix it to the page with the quarters slightly separated. This can't be beat for producing a dramatic long-distance effect!

Assembly Instructions

1. Using one 12" × 12" cardstock as your base attach one piece A to the page, placing it 2½" from the top and left edges. Attach remaining piece A to the page, placing it 2½" from the bottom and right edges.

2. Attach one piece B to the page placing it 2½" from the top and right edges. Attach remaining piece B to the page, placing it 2½" from the bottom and left edges.

3. Cut a 7" × 7" square from the center of piece C, leaving a 2" border. Attach piece C to the center of the page.

4. Attach photos, title, and journaling as desired.

Quartet–Pinwheel™

Paper Dimensions

A 7" × 5" (2)

B 5" × 7" (2)

C 1½" × 1½"

Assembly Instructions

1. Using one 12" × 12" cardstock as your base, attach one piece A to the top left corner of the page, keeping the edges flush. Attach remaining piece A to the bottom right corner of the page, keeping the edges flush.

2. Attach one piece B to the bottom left corner of the page keeping the edges flush. Attach remaining piece B to the top right corner of the page, keeping the edges flush.

3. Attach piece C centered between pieces A and B.

4. Attach photos, title, and journaling as desired.

Companion Layouts

8b

Master Pattern

A — Photo 1 6 × 4

B — Photo 2 4 × 6

C

A — Photo 1 6 × 4

B — Photo 2 4 × 6

DIMENSIONAL DELIGHT

Paper flowers take on a life of their own when they're allowed to really stand out! Try placing small 3-D foam squares under the petals, and watch these charmers pop off the page to make a memorable impression!

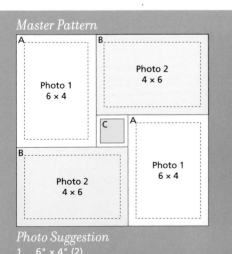

Photo Suggestion

1 6" × 4" (2)

2 4" × 6" (2)

Quartet–Perfect Square™

Paper Dimensions

A 6" × 6" (2)

B 5" × 5" (2)

C 5" × 5" (2)

Assembly Instructions

1. Using one 12" × 12" cardstock as your base, attach one piece A to the bottom left corner of the page, keeping the edges flush. Attach remaining piece A to the top right corner of the page, keeping the edges flush.

2. Attach one piece B to the center of each piece A.

3. Attach one piece C, placing it ½" from the top and left edges of the page. Attach remaining piece C, placing it ½" from the bottom and right edges of the page.

4. Attach photos, title, and journaling as desired.

Companion Layouts

This page is a right-side page only.

Master Pattern

C	A
Photo 1 4 × 4	B Photo 1 4 × 4
A B Photo 1 4 × 4	C Photo 1 4 × 4

Photo Suggestion

1 4" × 4" (4)

PERFECTLY PRETTY

Not all colors are created equal—but you can fix that! To make the colors in your photographs coordinate beautifully with the layout papers you're using, print your photos on matte paper and lightly color them with soft chalks until you achieve the desired shades. Your pictures and papers will coordinate perfectly every time!

Quartet–Columns™

EVERYTHING HINGES ON . . .

When it comes to journaling, you can make everything more interesting by using decorative hinges to attach journaling strips to a layout. You can either glue the strip firmly in place and attach a hinge to one end as an embellishment—or you can be a bit sneakier about it and attach just one end of the strip beneath the hinge, leaving space for a "hidden" message or journaling when the strip is lifted. It's up to you!

Master Pattern

A	B	C	
Photo 4½ × 2½	Photo 4½ × 2½	Photo 4½ × 2½	Photo 4½ × 2½

Photo Suggestion

1 4½" × 2½" (4)

Paper Dimensions

A   12" × 3"

B   12" × 3"

C   12" × 3"

Assembly Instructions

1. Using one 12" × 12" cardstock as your base, attach piece A to the left side of the page, keeping the edges flush.

2. Attach piece B directly to the right of piece A, keeping the edges flush.

3. Attach piece C directly to the right of piece B, keeping the edges flush.

4. Attach photos, title, and journaling as desired.

Companion Layouts

This page is a right-side page only.

Quartet–Panels™

Paper Dimensions

A   4" × 8"

B   4" × 4"

C   8" × 4"

D   7½" × 3½"

E   7" × 7"

Assembly Instructions

1. Using one 12" × 12" cardstock as your base, attach piece A to the bottom left corner of the page, keeping the edges flush.

2. Attach piece B to the bottom right corner of the page, keeping the edges flush.

3. Attach piece C to the top right corner of the page, keeping the edges flush.

4. Attach piece D to the center of piece C.

5. Attach piece E, placing it ½" from the top and left edges of the page.

6. Attach photos, title, and journaling as desired.

Companion Layouts

1b, 1d, 1j, 2h, 3d, 3e, 3f, 4j, 5g, 5h, 6i, 7f, 7j

TITLE EXPOSED

Tear your title up a little! Begin by stamping or adhering your title to the base cardstock and covering it with a patterned paper of your choice. Then, using a craft knife, make a thin cut all around the title. After removing the scrap of patterned paper covering the title, gently tear the edges back around the title, creating a weathered and adventurous look. It's a real attention-grabber!

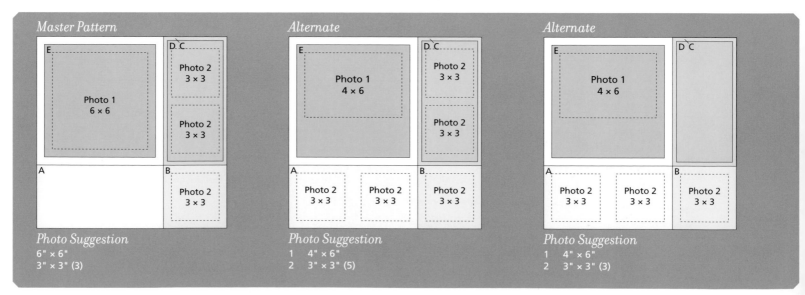

Master Pattern

E — Photo 1 6 × 6
D C — Photo 2 3 × 3 / Photo 2 3 × 3
A
B — Photo 2 3 × 3

Photo Suggestion
6" × 6"
3" × 3" (3)

Alternate

E — Photo 1 4 × 6
D C — Photo 2 3 × 3 / Photo 2 3 × 3
A — Photo 2 3 × 3 / Photo 2 3 × 3
B — Photo 2 3 × 3

Photo Suggestion
1   4" × 6"
2   3" × 3" (5)

Alternate

E — Photo 1 4 × 6
D C
A — Photo 2 3 × 3 / Photo 2 3 × 3
B — Photo 2 3 × 3

Photo Suggestion
1   4" × 6"
2   3" × 3" (3)

Quartet–Condensed™

Paper Dimensions

A   9" × 9"

Assembly Instructions

1.   Using one 12" × 12" cardstock as your base, attach piece A to the center of the page.

2.   Attach photos, title, and journaling as desired.

Companion Layouts

This page is a right-side page only.

Master Pattern

A	
Photo 1 4 × 4	Photo 1 4 × 4
Photo 1 4 × 4	Photo 1 4 × 4

Photo Suggestion

1   4" × 4" (4)

HANDWORK MEETS ARTWORK

A great way to add a homemade look to your layout is to crochet a simple chain with hemp or other fiber and attach it to the page as desired. Everyone will want to take a closer look!

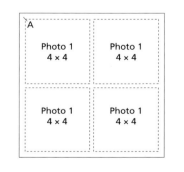

Quartet–Offset™

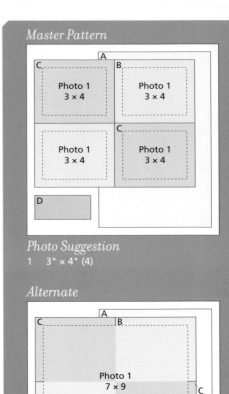

Master Pattern

Photo 1
3 × 4

Photo 1
3 × 4

Photo 1
3 × 4

Photo 1
3 × 4

A B C D

Photo Suggestion
1   3" × 4" (4)

Alternate

Photo 1
7 × 9

A B C D

Photo Suggestion
1   7" × 9"

Alternate

Photo 1
6½ × 4½

Photo 2
3 × 4

Photo 2
3 × 4

A B C D

Photo Suggestion
1   6½" × 4½"
2   3" × 4" (2)

Paper Dimensions

A   11" × 7"

B   8" × 10"

C   4" × 5" (2)

D   1½" × 3½"

Companion Layouts

This page is a right-side page only.

EVERYDAY INSPIRATION

Your pages will be truly unique if you incorporate everyday items in new ways to add interest—for example, here simple elements of the game "Life" are used to accessorize the page. Clearly inspired!

Assembly Instructions

1. Using one 12" × 12" cardstock as your base, attach piece A to the right side of the page, placing it ½" from the top, bottom, and right edges.

2. Attach piece B, placing it 1" from the top and ½" from the left edge of the page.

3. Attach one piece C to the top left corner of piece B, keeping the edges flush. Attach remaining piece C to the bottom right corner of piece B, keeping the edges flush.

4. Attach piece D, placing it ½" from the left edge and 1" from the bottom of the page.

5. Attach photos, title, and journaling as desired.

Quartet–Jigsaw™

Paper Dimensions

A 8" × 6" (2)

B 7" × 5" (2)

C 3" × 5" (2)

Assembly Instructions

1. Using one 12" × 12" cardstock as your base, attach one piece A to the bottom left corner of the page, keeping the edges flush. Attach remaining piece A to the top right corner of the page, keeping the edges flush.

2. Attach one piece B to the center of each piece A.

3. Attach one piece C, placing it ½" from the top and left edges of the page. Attach remaining piece C, placing it ½" from the bottom and right edges of the page.

4. Attach photos, title, and journaling as desired.

Companion Layouts

8h

AGE IS BEAUTY

Combining cocoa-colored and lighter brown inks will age and distress the edges of a page or photo beautifully. Try swiping across one stamp pad and then the other, or combine re-inkers in a craft jar and use a sponge or other texturing tool to distress the edges.

Master Pattern

C — Photo 2 — 2½ × 4½

A — B — Photo 1 — 6 × 4

A — B — Photo 1 — 6 × 4

C — Photo 2 — 2½ × 4½

Photo Suggestion

1   6" × 4" (2)

2   2½" × 4½" (2)

Quartet–In Balance™

Paper Dimensions

A   11" × 8½"

B   6" × 7½"

C   5½" × 4"

D   3½" × 8½"

Assembly Instructions

1. Using one 12" × 12" cardstock as your base, attach piece A, placing it ½" from the top, bottom, and left edges.

2. Attach piece B, placing it ½" from the bottom and side edges of piece A.

3. Attach piece C to piece B, placing it ¼" from the top and left edges.

4. Attach piece D, placing it 1" from the top and right edges of the page.

5. Attach photos, title, and journaling as desired.

Companion Layouts

This page is a right-side page only.

Master Pattern

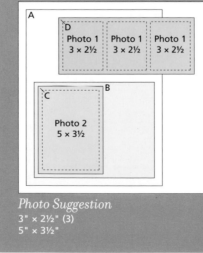

D	
Photo 1 3 × 2½	Photo 1 3 × 2½	Photo 1 3 × 2½

C

Photo 2
5 × 3½

Photo Suggestion

3" × 2½" (3)

5" × 3½"

RIBBON IMAGES

Decorative ribbon can be used as inspiration for your background paper. Use the design elements in the ribbon and recreate the pattern on your paper for a coordinating layout every time!

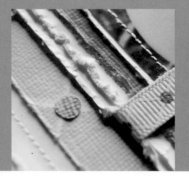

Quartet–Sliding™

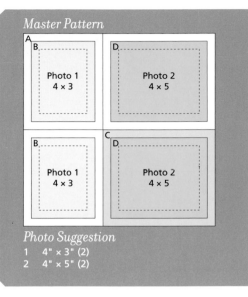

Master Pattern

A
B
Photo 1
4 × 3

D
Photo 2
4 × 5

B
Photo 1
4 × 3

C
D
Photo 2
4 × 5

Photo Suggestion
1 4" × 3" (2)
2 4" × 5" (2)

PATTERN YOUR PAPER WITH RIBBON

You can easily create your own original patterned paper design by adhering strips of coordinating ribbon to cardstock. Your layout will say "brilliant" to everyone who sees it!

Paper Dimensions

A   6" × 5"

B   5" × 4" (2)

C   6" × 7"

D   5" × 6" (2)

Assembly Instructions

1. Using one 12" × 12" cardstock as your base, attach piece A to the top left corner of the page, keeping the edges flush.

2. Attach one piece B to the center of piece A.

3. Attach remaining piece B, placing it ½" from the bottom and left edges of the page.

4. Attach piece C to the bottom right corner of the page, keeping the edges flush.

5. Attach one piece D to the center of piece C.

6. Attach remaining piece D, placing it ½" from the top and right edges of the page.

7. Attach photos, title, and journaling as desired.

Companion Layouts

8j (rotated)

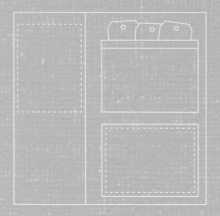

Treasure Pocket™

Ashley is pure muscle in more ways than one. She's my eldest child: my partner and inspiration through many challenging years. Ashley reminds me that strength is the blessing of trial, and that nothing is as beautiful as determination. What a journey we have walked together!

This Treasure Pocket pattern is ideal for preserving your journey—not just in photos, but with journaled tags, tickets, mementos, and the other keepsakes that make up real life. Don't set those pieces aside; incorporate them into your layouts! Flex your creative muscle and tackle the tough stuff when you scrapbook. Life is strong; your layouts should be, too.

9a • *Treasure Pocket–Basic*™

Paper Dimensions

A 6½" × 12"

B 6" × 12"

Assembly Instructions

1. Using one 12" × 12" cardstock as your base, attach piece A to the bottom of the page, adhering only the bottom and side edges, in order to form a pocket.

2. Attach piece B to the bottom of piece A, keeping the edges flush.

3. Insert memorabilia into pocket.

4. Attach photos, title, and journaling as desired.

Master Pattern

A
B

Photo Suggestion
As desired

Companion Layouts

This page is a right-side page only.

9b • *Treasure Pocket–Main*™

Paper Dimensions

A 12" × 3"

B 4" × 9"

C ½" × 9"

D 5½" × 7½"

Assembly Instructions

1. Using one 12" × 12" cardstock as your base, attach piece A to the left side of the page, keeping the edges flush.

2. Attach piece B to the bottom right corner of the page, adhering only the bottom and side edges in order to form a pocket.

3. Attach piece C to the top of piece B, keeping the side edges flush.

4. Attach piece D, placing it ¾" from the top and right edges of the page.

5. Insert memorabilia into pocket.

6. Attach photos, title, and journaling as desired.

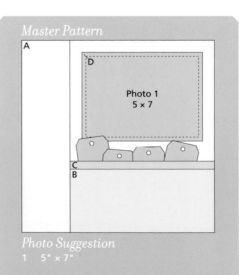

Master Pattern

A
D

Photo 1
5 × 7

C
B

Photo Suggestion
1   5" × 7"

Companion Layouts

1d, 1e, 1i, 1j, 2k, 3b, 4d, 6h, 7f, 8f, 9a, 9c, 10b

Treasure Pocket–Accent™

Paper Dimensions

A   12" × 4½"

B   4½" × 6" (2)

C   ½" × 6"

Assembly Instructions

1. Using one 12" × 12" cardstock as your base, attach piece A to the left side of the page, keeping the edges flush.

2. Attach pieces B, placing them ½" from the bottom and side edges and ¾" from each other, adhering only the bottom and side edges of upper piece B, in order to form a pocket.

3. Attach piece C to the top of upper piece B, keeping the side edges flush.

4. Insert memorabilia into pocket.

5. Attach photos, title, and journaling as desired.

Master Pattern

A

Photo 1
5½ × 4

C
B

B

Photo 2
4 × 5½

Photo Suggestion
1   5½" × 4"
2   4" × 5½"

Companion Layouts

This page is a right-side page only.

Treasure Pocket–Folio™

Paper Dimensions

A   4" × 12"

B   ½" × 12"

C   8" × 6"

D   7½" × 5½"

Assembly Instructions

1. Using one 12" × 12" file folder as your base, attach piece A to the top of the page, keeping the edges flush, trim as desired.

2. Attach piece B to piece A, placing it 3" from the top, keeping the side edges flush.

3. Attach piece C to the bottom left corner of the page, keeping the edges flush.

4. Attach piece D, placing it ¼" from the bottom and right edges of the page.

5. Insert memorabilia into pocket.

6. Attach photos, title, and journaling as desired.

Master Pattern

A

B

C

D

Photo 1
7 × 5

Photo Suggestion
1   7" × 5"

Companion Layouts

This page is a right-side page only.

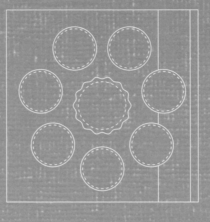

Sampler™

My son Jared taught me to dig a little deeper, to try a little harder in everything I did. As a child, he adored soccer—he always had the drive to win, but his primary motive was self-challenge.

The Sampler patterns bring out that same striving in me: pushing my own creativity just a little bit further to set design trends rather than merely react to them. Take this Flower pattern for example: Who would have thought you could incorporate eight photos on a single page and still achieve visual balance? With determination and a little confidence, you'll always win, regardless of the game.

10a • Sampler–Nine-Photo Quilt™

Paper Dimensions

A   11" × 11"

B   3½" × 3½" (5)

C   3½" × 3½" (4)

Assembly Instructions

1. Using one 12" × 12" cardstock as your base, attach piece A to the center of the page.

2. Attach pieces B in all four corners and the center of piece A, spacing them evenly from the edges of piece A and from each other.

3. Attach pieces C in between the pieces B, spacing them evenly.

4. Attach photos, title, and journaling as desired.

Companion Layouts

This page is a right-side page only.

Master Pattern

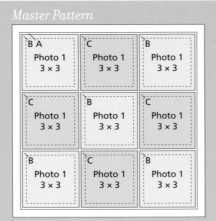

B A	C	B
Photo 1 3 × 3	Photo 1 3 × 3	Photo 1 3 × 3
C	B	C
Photo 1 3 × 3	Photo 1 3 × 3	Photo 1 3 × 3
B	C	B
Photo 1 3 × 3	Photo 1 3 × 3	Photo 1 3 × 3

Photo Suggestion

1   3" × 3" (4–9)

10b • Sampler–Flower™

Paper Dimensions

A   12" × 2"

B   3½" circle

C   2¾" circle (7)

Assembly Instructions

1. Using one 12" × 12" cardstock as your base, attach piece A, placing it ½" from the right edge of the page, keeping the top and bottom flush.

2. Attach piece B to the center of the page.

3. Attach pieces C around piece B, spacing them evenly from the edges of the page, piece B, and each other.

4. Attach photos, title, and journaling as desired.

Companion Layouts

This page is a right-side page only.

Master Pattern

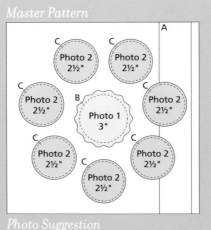

C — Photo 2 2½"
C — Photo 2 2½"
C — Photo 2 2½"
C — Photo 2 2½"
B — Photo 1 3"
C — Photo 2 2½"
C — Photo 2 2½"
C — Photo 2 2½"
A

Photo Suggestion

1   3" circle

2   2½" circles (7)

Sampler–Mix™

Paper Dimensions

A   3½" × 11½"

B   7½" × 11½"

C   7" × 3½"

D   1½" × 7"

Assembly Instructions

1. Using one 12" × 12" cardstock as your base, attach piece A, placing it ½" from the top and ¼" from the side edges.

2. Attach piece B, placing it ¼" from the bottom and side edges of the page.

3. Attach piece C, placing it ¼" from the top and left edges of piece B.

4. Attach piece D, placing it ¼" from the bottom and right edges of piece B.

5. Attach photos, title, and journaling as desired.

Companion Layouts

This page is a right-side page only.

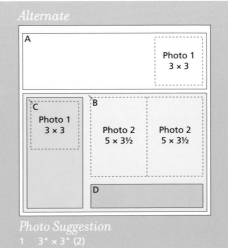

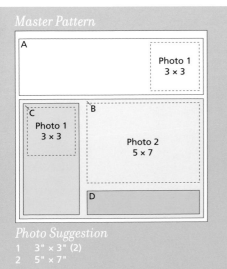

Master Pattern

A

Photo 1
3 × 3

C
Photo 1
3 × 3

B

Photo 2
5 × 7

D

Photo Suggestion
1   3" × 3" (2)
2   5" × 7"

Alternate

A

Photo 1
3 × 3

Photo 1
3 × 3

Photo 1
3 × 3

C
Photo 1
3 × 3

B

Photo 2
5 × 7

Photo 1
3 × 3

D

Photo Suggestion
1   3" × 3" (5)
2   5" × 7"

Alternate

A

Photo 1
3 × 3

C
Photo 1
3 × 3

B

Photo 2
5 × 3½

Photo 2
5 × 3½

D

Photo Suggestion
1   3" × 3" (2)
2   5" × 3½" (2)

Sampler–Pieced™

Paper Dimensions

A   11" × 11"

B   6" × 4"

C   1¼" × 2½" (2)

D   3" × 2½"

E   2⅞" × 3" (2)

F   2½" × 2½"

G   1" × 2½"

H   3¾" × 3½" (2)

Companion Layouts

This page is a right-side page only.

STITCHED PHOTO MATS

For a twist to photo matting, use the photo and stitching to create a unique border. Cut the photo the size of your paper dimension, then sew a ¼" border around the entire photo.

Master Pattern

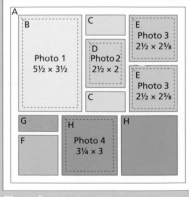

Photo Suggestion

1   5½" × 3½"

2   2½" × 2"

3   2½" × 2⅜" (2)

4   3¼" × 3"

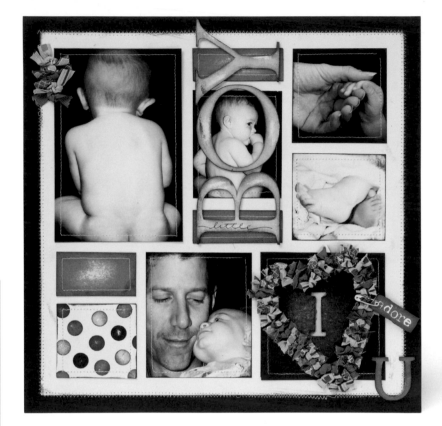

Assembly Instructions

1. Using one 12" × 12" cardstock as your base, attach piece A to the center of the page.

2. Attach piece B to piece A, placing it ½" from the top and left edges.

3. Attach one piece C ¼" to the right of piece B, keeping the top edges aligned. Attach remaining piece C ¼" to the right of piece B, keeping the bottom edges aligned.

4. Attach piece D ¼" to the right of piece B, centered top to bottom between pieces C.

5. Attach pieces E to piece A, placing them ½" from the top, ½" from the right, and ¼" from each other.

6. Attach piece F to piece A, placing it ½" from the bottom and left edges.

7. Attach piece G to piece A, placing it ½" from the right and ¼" above piece F.

8. Attach pieces H to piece A, placing them ½" from the bottom, ½" from the right, and ¼" from each other.

9. Attach photos, title, and journaling as desired.

Master Pattern

B A Photo 1 3 × 3	D Photo 1 3 × 3	C Photo 1 3 × 3
D Photo 1 3 × 3	B Photo 1 3 × 3	D Photo 1 3 × 3
C Photo 1 3 × 3	D Photo 1 3 × 3	B Photo 1 3 × 3

Photo Suggestion

1   3" × 3" (4–9)

TYING ONE ON

You can create a tied quilt look by literally "tying" the squares on a layout with yarn or other fibers.

Assembly Instructions

1. Using one 12" × 12" cardstock as your base, attach piece A to the center of the page.

2. Attach pieces B in the top left corner, bottom right corner, and center of piece A, placing them ¼" from the edges of piece A.

3. Attach pieces C to the top right and bottom left corners of piece A, placing them ¼" from the edges of piece A.

4. Attach pieces D in between the pieces B and C, keeping the edges flush.

5. Attach photos, title, and journaling as desired.

Paper Dimensions

A   11" × 11"

B   3½" × 3½" (3)

C   3½" × 3½" (2)

D   3½" × 3½" (4)

Companion Layouts

This page is a right-side page only.

Sampler–Captivating Corners™

BUTTON UP

Want to give your buttons a weathered and distressed look? Try sanding them and sponging them lightly with your choice of ink. It's easy to do, and it adds all kinds of fun texture and character to the button!

Master Pattern

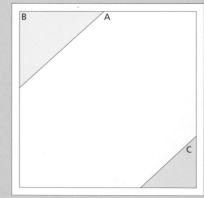

Photo Suggestion
Various

Paper Dimensions

A   11" × 11"

B   4¾" × 5½" (cut diagonally)

C   3¼" × 3½" (cut diagonally)

Companion Layouts

This page is a right-side page only.

Assembly Instructions

1. Using one 12" × 12" cardstock as your base, attach piece A to the center of the page.

2. Cut piece B in half diagonally. Attach one piece to the top left corner of piece A, keeping the edges flush.

3. Cut piece C in half diagonally. Attach one piece C to the bottom right corner of piece A, keeping the edges flush.

4. Attach photos, title, and journaling as desired.

Sampler–Collage™

Paper Dimensions

A 11" × 11"

B 3¾" × 3¾" (4)

C 3" circle

D 4¼" × 4¼"

E 3½" circle

F 2½" circle

G 3¼" × 5¼"

Assembly Instructions

1. Using one 12" × 12" cardstock as your base, attach piece A to the center of the page.

2. Attach pieces B, C, D, E, F, and G to piece A in a random order at complementary angles.

3. Attach photos, title, and journaling as desired.

Master Pattern

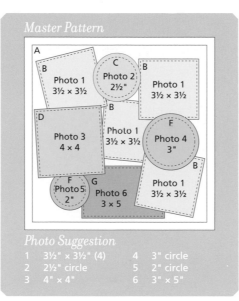

| A |
B	C Photo 2 2½"	B
Photo 1 3½ × 3½		Photo 1 3½ × 3½
D	B	
Photo 3 4 × 4	Photo 1 3½ × 3½	F Photo 4 3"
F Photo 5 2"	G Photo 6 3 × 5	Photo 1 3½ × 3½	B

Photo Suggestion

1	3½" × 3½" (4)	4	3" circle
2	2½" circle	5	2" circle
3	4" × 4"	6	3" × 5"

Companion Layouts

This page is a right-side page only.

Sampler–Calendar™

Paper Dimensions

A 11" × 11"

B 2" × 10¼"

C ½" × 10¼"

D 1¼" × 1¼" (28–31)

Assembly Instructions

1. Using one 12" × 12" cardstock as your base, attach piece A to the center of the page.

2. Attach piece B to the top of piece A, placing it ¼" from the top and ⅜" from the left and right edges.

3. Attach piece C ¼" below piece B and ⅜" from the left and right edges of piece A.

4. Attach pieces D in rows of seven, placing them ⅜" from the bottom, left, and right edges of the page and ¼" from each other.

5. Attach title, and journaling as desired.

Master Pattern

B A

C

D	D	D	D	D	D	D
D	D	D	D	D	D	D
D	D	D	D	D	D	D
D	D	D	D	D	D	D
D	D	D	D	D	D	D

Photo Suggestion

As desired

Companion Layouts

This page is a right-side page only.

Sampler™